on track ...

Bruce Springsteen

1973-1987

every album, every song

David Starkey

sonicbondpublishing.com

Sonicbond Publishing Limited
www.sonicbondpublishing.co.uk
Email: info@sonicbondpublishing.co.uk

First Published in the United Kingdom 2026
First Published in the United States 2026

British Library Cataloguing in Publication Data:
A Catalogue record for this book is available from the British Library

Typeset in ITC Garamond Std & ITC Avant Garde Gothic
Printed and bound in England

Graphic design and typesetting: Full Moon Media

Follow us on social media:
Twitter: https://twitter.com/SonicbondP
Instagram: www.instagram.com/sonicbondpublishing_/
Facebook: www.facebook.com/SonicbondPublishing/

Linktree QR code:

on track ...
Bruce Springsteen
1973–1987

every album, every song

David Starkey

sonicbondpublishing.com

For Sandy

Oh, come take my hand,
we're riding out tonight to case the promised land ...
'Thunder Road'

Acknowledgements

There is no shortage of material about Bruce Springsteen and his work. Perhaps Elvis, The Beatles and Dylan have had more words written about them, but it's a close race, and critical and fan writing about Springsteen is enormous and ongoing.

When in doubt, I turned to *Born To Run*, Bruce Springsteen's 500-page 2016 autobiography, which does an excellent job of presenting him as he wants to be remembered, and also does a pretty good job of explaining when and how his perspectives on writing and performing his work shifted over time. There is, however, less material about the composition of individual songs than an *On Track* author might want, and I often turned to *Songs*, a collection of Springsteen's lyrics, with commentary by the Boss. For other first-person accounts, I looked at interviews Springsteen has given over the decades, many of them collected in *Talk About A Dream: The Essential Interviews Of Bruce Springsteen*, edited by Christopher Phillips and Louis P. Masur, and *Springsteen On Springsteen: Interviews, Speeches, And Encounters*, edited by Jeff Burger. And *Rolling Stone* magazine has been an avid supporter from the beginning: its archives contain a wealth of material.

While I didn't always agree with their interpretations of individual songs, I am grateful for all the legwork French authors Philippe Margotin and Jean-Michel Guesdon did in compiling primary and secondary sources in their monumental *Bruce Springsteen: All The Songs, The Story Behind Every Track*. In *Bruce Springsteen: The Stories Behind The Songs*, Rolling Stone journalist Brian Hiatt travels the same ground, with sometimes different interpretations of the music. Clinton Heylin's *Springsteen Song By Song: A Critical Look* was another useful source: Heylin zeroes in on facts about the songs' compositions and mostly leaves the interpretations to others. Rob Kirkpatrick's *Magic In The Night: The Words And Music Of Bruce Springsteen* is another excellent and comprehensive source.

My former editor, the wonderous June Skinner Sawyers, has authored or edited several important books about Springsteen, including *Tougher Than The Rest: 100 Best Bruce Springsteen Songs* and *Racing In The Street: The Bruce Springsteen Reader*. Dave Marsh's *Born To Run*, *Glory Days* and *Two Hearts* were occasionally helpful, and Warren Zanes' *Deliver Me From Nowhere: The Making Of Bruce Springsteen's Nebraska* is an essential read for those writing about the Boss's sixth album. In regard to *Born To Run*, ditto for Peter Ames Carlin's *Tonight In Jungleland: The Making Of Born To Run*. It's also interesting to hear early manager Mike Appel's perspective in Marc Eliot's *Thunder Road*.

Fans write frequently, and often quite well, about their hero. There's the Greasy Lake Community (with its nod to 'Spirit In The Night'), Backstreets. com, Letters to You and Blogness on the Edge of Town, among others. Ken Rosen's *E Street Blog* is especially insightful and detailed, with plenty of links to music and videos.

I'm also grateful for the many conversations I've had about Springsteen with friends, especially Barbara Bell – 43 concerts and counting – the always thoughtful David Sherman and my ever-astute wife, Sandy.

Finally, thank you to Stephen Lambe and the folks at Sonicbond Publishing. Talking Heads, the subject of my previous *On Track* volume, make a very different kind of music than Bruce Springsteen, but I learned a lot from that book – and from Stephen – about how to identify the most important elements of a song and to bring it to life in the fewest possible words.

on track ...
Bruce Springsteen
1973-1987

Contents

Introduction: Tougher Than The Rest

Anyone writing about Bruce Springsteen is bound to wonder, what can I say that hasn't already been said?

The answer, for me, has been to do my best to take a fresh, open and critical look at creative work that has accompanied me through the world from my pre-teen years into my 60s. When analyzing Springsteen's music, I often relied on my 47 years of playing in rock bands, and when analyzing his lyrics, I drew on my training and career as a poet. Poets and songwriters are different creatures to be sure – the former often thinking first of the page, the latter always relying on the sung voice and musical accompaniment – but Springsteen has been rightly hailed as one of our great lyricists, so I have examined his words with the careful attention they deserve.

That said, Springsteen's lyrics, even in his early, most vibrant years, are not universally excellent. At his best, on *Born To Run*, *Darkness On The Edge Of Town* and parts of *The River*, Springsteen uses searing, unforgettable imagery with great concision, even when the tracks, like 'Thunder Road' and 'Jungleland', are far longer than the average pop song. At other times, however, with the 'party' songs on *The River* as good examples – 'Cadillac Ranch', 'I'm A Rocker', 'You Can Look (But You Better Not Touch)' – Springsteen's work is more memorable for its energy and fun than for its lyrical inventiveness.

Moreover, while the music accompanying these words can be quite complex and moving, even when it is simple, the Boss is not above relying on the same I-IV-V chord progression that can make some songs – the three just mentioned above come to mind – sound rather, well, less than extraordinary.

This book, therefore, is not another hagiography of Bruce Springsteen. There are plenty of those already. Instead, I try to offer a careful, measured look at the work of one of the great American singer-songwriters of the last century. Yes, his output is in many ways unparalleled. But it is not perfect. No artist can make that claim about their work, and only the laziest of critics would accept such a claim anyway.

Of course, one of the reasons Springsteen's output is likely to be uneven or sometimes repetitive is that he is one of the most prolific recording artists in American history. The singles and albums he released from 1973 to 1987 do not represent all the work he recorded at that time. Far from it. In 1998, he released *Tracks*, a four-CD set of 66 outtakes, B-sides and alternate versions of his early music. In 2010, he released *The Promise*, a two-CD collection of 22 songs recorded around the time of *Darkness On The Edge Of Town*. In 2015, he released *The Ties That Bind: The River Collection*, a four-CD, three-DVD exploration of *The River*, which includes 25 unreleased songs. And in 2025, he released an even larger volume of new/old material. *Tracks II: The Lost Albums* contains 83 songs from the time between *Nebraska* and 2018, with the tracks organized into seven unreleased albums. And as I was writing this book, he released *Nebraska '82*, a four-disc set which includes the long-rumored 'electric *Nebraska*' versions of the songs on his first true solo album.

The Boss, in short, is a songwriting and song-recording machine.

The material Springsteen offered for sale long after he originally recorded it deserves an *On Track* volume of its own, and we may well see such a volume in the future. In the meantime, this book's focus is on the music actually released during the time period being covered – including the B-sides of singles not included on albums. When appropriate, I will make reference to recordings made available to the public years later, but my attention will stay on what might be called the 'canonical' works of 1973 to 1987. This material, more than 150 songs, is already a substantial body of work to cover in a short book such as this one. Trying to discuss both the officially released music and the songs that dropped years later would result in nothing but a cursory overview of all the music. Instead, my goal is to zero in on what makes each song unique, giving every track from *Asbury Park* to *Tunnel Of Love*, along with the B-sides of singles from those albums, as much attention as space allows.

Focusing largely on the nine albums released during this time makes sense. While casual listeners may know hits like 'Hungry Heart', 'Born In The U.S.A.' and 'Dancing In The Dark', Springsteen has always been a maker of *albums*. In fact, to date, he has never had a number one single in the US or the UK. In his autobiography, *Born To Run*, he talks about agonizing over which material to leave in and what to leave out, often extending the process of making an album by many months as he whittles his choices down to the songs that he loves most *and* that work together best as a unified whole.

And what a trove of music that is! For my money, *Born To Run* and *Darkness On The Edge Of Town* are two of the greatest rock 'n' roll albums ever recorded. They are high-water marks showing a gifted lyricist and composer working with passion and poise in conjunction with a remarkable group of musicians. Two other albums from this period – *The River* and *Born In The U.S.A.* – are also among the treasures of American popular music in the last half of the 20th century. The four other studio albums under discussion range from the early but not fully realized promise of *Greetings From Asbury Park, N.J.* and *The Wild, The Innocent & The E Street Shuffle* to the stark acoustic portraits of *Nebraska*, and the synth-heavy and often underappreciated *Tunnel Of Love*. *Bruce Springsteen And The E Street Band Live/1975-1985*, originally released as a five-LP boxed extravaganza, gives a foretaste of the numerous live albums to follow, including the many dozens of recordings of individual shows from across his career available on live. brucespringsteen.net.

More Balzac than Flaubert – concerned with expressing big feelings and building an expansive picture of his community, rather than commenting invisibly from the shadows – Springsteen delves into many lives and experiences, with his characters' worlds often interconnected through geography and circumstance. He has a fecund lyrical and musical imagination, yet over the years, Springsteen has returned to the same themes – blue-collar work and unemployment, cars and the open road, family, the highs of falling in love and the lows of soured relationships – and done so in songs that range from folk to full-on large band spectaculars, but which always sound of a piece with his overall aesthetic: the bar band king who also loves Bob Dylan and always wants to connect with his audience, even when, as on *Nebraska*, he pushes them outside their comfort zone.

Bruce Frederick Joseph Springsteen was born in Long Branch, New Jersey, on 23 September 1949, and grew up in nearby Freehold, a town in the central part of the state between Trenton on the west and Asbury Park on the east. It's less than an hour south of New York City, but a world away from the metropolis. While Freehold offered factory jobs to its working-class citizens, it was set in the midst of the countryside, a fact which explains a great deal about the Boss's frequent journeyings between urban and rural life in his songs.

In his autobiography, *Born To Run*, Springsteen describes his family life as dominated by the menacing broodings of his father, Douglas, aka 'Dutch', and the often-inadequate role played by his mother, Adele (neé Zerilli) – always faithful first to her husband – at mitigating the darkness emanating from the kitchen table, where Doug silently chain-smoked and drank beer after beer. Bruce was the oldest of three children and was treated like a king by his paternal grandmother; his two younger sisters appear to have played a relatively small role in his growing-up years.

More impactful was the cultural influence of the two sides of his family: Irish-American on his father's side, and Italian-American on his mother's. Interestingly, the surname Springsteen is Dutch, with Springsteen's ancestors going back to colonial America. But it was his doting grandmother, Martha O'Hagan, whom the singer connected with most, decades later appearing on the PBS Documentary *Faces Of America* to trace his ancestry back to County Kildare.

Despite all the talk in his autobiography about his Irish and Italian roots, the more 'neutral' European name of Springsteen probably worked to his advantage in the show business of the 1970s and 1980s. It's hard to imagine Bruce O'Hagan or Bruce Zerilli connecting with quite as wide a swathe of the American populace.

In any event, Springsteen's working-class Catholic childhood, with his mother, a legal secretary, often the chief breadwinner, and his father, who was later diagnosed as bipolar, moving in and out of demanding and unsatisfying blue-collar jobs, profoundly affected his art. Springsteen wanted out of Freehold badly, and inspired by seeing both Elvis Presley and The Beatles on *The Ed Sullivan Show*, in 1964 he bought his first guitar for less than 20 dollars at the Western Auto appliance store. After a steep early learning curve – it turned out you had to actually *tune* the instrument – the young musician graduated to a $60 Kent electric guitar, and soon he had formed a group, the Castiles, a cover band which rehearsed in the rundown home of a sympathetic older couple.

The Castiles soon migrated to Asbury Park on the Jersey Shore and became part of the area's surf culture. A photograph of the group performing at the Ferndock Surf Shop (Sales & Rentals) shows them with Beatles haircuts and surf-inspired duds.

Eventually, like most garage bands dependent on hyper-local gigs (the Elks Club, the Union Hall, the Church basement), the Castiles broke up. This was 1968, when, as Springsteen writes in *Born To Run*, 'hard-rocking psychedelic blues trios had superseded the beat groups. The era of the guitar god was in full swing.' Accordingly, Earth was Springsteen's next band, although at the time he was more preoccupied with dodging the draft through the time-honored method of acting 'the mumbling, bumbling, swishing, don't-give-a-fuck-about-orders freak on STP, LSD and anything you can get your hands on.' The ruse worked, and the man who became a champion of veterans had his 1-Y mental deferment, though, as he says, 'As I grew older, I sometimes wonder who went in my place.'

Springsteen's next gig was as the singer and lead guitarist of a band initially called Child, but which later changed its name to Steel Mill. Sidemen included future E Street Band members drummer Vini Lopez, organist Danny Federici and guitarist Steven Van Zandt. A live album of the group was released in 2017, and they are clearly a more-than-competent blues-rock jam band. The songs are eight, ten, 15 and even 20 minutes long, and while Springsteen was never going to rival Hendrix or Clapton, he clearly gained some valuable experience playing blues scales for long minutes on end. While Steel Mill was popular in New Jersey and, oddly, Richmond, Virginia, opening for acts like Ike and Tina Turner and Black Sabbath, they didn't take hold nationally, and they played their final show in January 1971.

The next few years found Springsteen searching for a sound and a voice. He formed the Bruce Springsteen Band, but also began writing Dylan-influenced acoustic material, which he performed solo in coffee houses and small bars in New Jersey and New York City. In May 1972, Springsteen, through the pushiness of his new manager, Mike Appel, had a very successful audition in front of the legendary John Hammond. This was a turning point for the young musician. As he writes in his autobiography: 'We'd climbed to the heavens and spoken to the gods, who told us we were spitting thunder and throwing thunderbolts!' Springsteen signed with Columbia and gathered together a group of musicians with whom, from June to October 1972, he would record his first album: *Greetings From Asbury Park, N.J.*

Greetings From Asbury Park, N.J. (1973)

Personnel:

Bruce Springsteen: lead vocals, acoustic guitar, electric guitar, harmonica, congas, handclaps, bass guitar on 'Blinded By The Light' and 'Spirit In The Night', piano on 'Spirit In The Night'

Clarence Clemons: saxophone, backing vocals, handclaps on 'Blinded By The Light' and 'Spirit In The Night'

Vini Lopez: drums, backing vocals, handclaps

David Sancious: piano, Hammond organ, keyboards

Garry Tallent: bass guitar

Harold Wheeler: piano on 'Blinded By The Light' and 'Spirits In The Night'

Recorded at 914 Sound, Blauvelt, New York, between 7 June and 26 October 1972

Producers: Mike Appel and Jim Cretocos

Release date: 5 January 1973

Running time: 37:08

Label: Columbia

Album charts: US: 60, UK: 41 (1985)

Speaking to Jann Wenner of *Rolling Stone*, Springsteen remarked, 'I always say [Bob Dylan] is the father of my country. He initially provided me with a picture of a country that I recognized. One that feels real, that feels like the truth. My early-20s writing, certainly *Greetings From Asbury Park*, was influenced by Dylan, though if you go back to it now, it had its quirks and that made it sort of its own record.' That is, indeed, a good way to approach Springsteen's first album: heavily influenced by Dylan, especially in the lyrics, but with Springsteen doing his best to push past that obvious inspiration.

According to his autobiography, the songs for *Asbury Park* were largely written in the back of a former beauty salon beneath his Asbury Park apartment: 'I had an old Aeolian spinet piano my aunt had given me, and amid the hairdryers and washing sinks, I wrote the songs.' In later interviews, he would claim that this was the only time he wrote the words first and the music afterwards, and that makes sense, for the lyrics are bountiful and overflowing – sometimes too much so.

Musically, the acoustic songs do resonate with *Bringing It All Back Home*-era Dylan, but the electric songs are something altogether different, reflecting Springsteen's love of soul music and his long apprenticeship in Jersey Shore bar bands.

Springsteen's back-up band did not officially become the E Street Band until September 1974, but here they are at the beginning of his official recording career, ready to rock 'n' roll. On the bottom end, there is bassist Gary Tallent, the only member of the original lineup still playing with the band as these words are written, 53 years after *Asbury Park* was recorded. In *Born To Run*, Springsteen describes Tallent's playing as 'invisible, transparent, rising up out of your dreams, creating a bed for them to lie on rather than intruding upon them. Then, when you go to the bottom, he's always there. No show pony, he's in the great tradition of the silent men drawn to the bass guitar.'

Vini 'Mad Dog' Lopez is on drums, and his nickname suggests not only his offstage behavior, but his approach to drumming, which is quite different from Tallent's near-invisibility. Unlike the ever-steady Max Weinberg, who would replace Lopez in 1974, Mad Dog brings a flash and flair to the job that were well-suited to Springsteen's first two albums.

David Sancious is featured on organ and piano, duties that would later be split in the E Street Band by Danny Federici and Roy Bittan. One of the few African American members to be part of the ensemble, Sancious was classically trained and plays with the style and grace of an accomplished jazz pianist. Incidentally, the E Street Band takes its name from the street in Belmar, New Jersey, where the band used to practice, in a garage owned by Sancious's mother. Ultimately, Sancious's improvisational skills clashed with the sound the band leader wanted, with Springsteen preferring the straightforward rock 'n' roll keyboards of Federici and Bittan, but Sancious's contributions to this album and its follow-up should not be underestimated.

Finally, there is Clarence Clemons on saxophone. Though Springsteen acknowledges that the two men did not spend a great deal of time together offstage – Clemons's life was just too chaotic – onstage, he considered the saxophonist a brother in arms. That's not quite yet his role in *Asbury Park*, but when he does appear, on 'Blinded By The Light' and 'Spirits In The Night', his presence is powerful indeed.

As with many a great artist's first album, the recording conditions for *Greetings From Asbury Park, N.J.* were not ideal. 914 Sound Recording Studios was in Blauvelt, New York, a small town on the Tappan Zee, built on the site of an old garage. Its leaky roof notwithstanding, Springsteen saw advantages in their out-of-the-way location: 'Here, we could get a cheap recording rate [and] carry on as we pleased out of sight of the nosy record company bigwigs, who might be too curious about how their money was being spent.' $40,000 had been allotted for the recording, but in the end, only $11,000 would be required, an atypical outcome for the famously perfectionist Springsteen.

The album was produced by Mike Appel, Springsteen's pugnacious manager, and Appel's publishing and management partner Jim Cretocos. Perhaps previously better known as a songwriting team, Appel and Cretocos, along with Wes Farrell, had penned five songs for the Partridge Family, including the US top ten hit 'Doesn't Somebody Want To Be Wanted'. Appel insisted on bringing in his own recording engineer, Louis Lahav, but Columbia wanted to use their union engineer. Ultimately, Appel prevailed, with the union engineer getting paid to sit in the back of the studio, away from the controls, and read the newspaper.

When the 'completed' album was brought to Columbia Records president Clive Davis, he did not hear a hit, telling his newly signed artist to go out and write one. In a few days, Springsteen dutifully wrote two of his most recognizable songs – 'Blinded By The Light' and 'Spirit In The Night' – thankfully leaving three verbose acoustic songs – 'Jazz Musician', 'Arabian Nights' and 'Visitation At Fort Horn' – on the cutting room floor.

The album cover represented another struggle between Columbia's vision of who Springsteen should be and who he felt he actually was. In a 1975 interview with Ray Coleman of *Melody Maker*, Springsteen says he insisted on the album title, and the cover art, a postcard with nostalgic images from Asbury Park inside the body of the title's letters – an idea based on an actual postcard Springsteen brought to Columbia's design team. On the original LP, the 'postcard' is attached to the left side of the cover and opens up to reveal a picture of Springsteen as the stamp, with the album information in the area where the message would normally be written. The cover beneath the postcard foldout is black, with both front and back sides covered by lyrics in a tiny white font. Clearly, the listener was meant to appreciate Springsteen's gifts as a writer.

Greetings From Asbury Park, N.J. was released in early January 1973. Artists with top ten albums at the time included America, Cat Stevens and Carole King. It was a good time to be a singer-songwriter, which was why Columbia had been so insistent on pushing Springsteen into this role, but it was an awkward fit: Springsteen's purely acoustic numbers like 'Mary Queen Of Arkansas' and 'The Angel' were never going to be top 40 material. It was rockers like the two new songs, along with 'Growin' Up' and 'For You', that showed potential as radio-friendly material.

The reception to the album was mixed. Writing in *Rolling Stone*, Lester Bangs was not entirely enthusiastic: 'Old Bruce makes a point of letting us know that he's from one of the scuzziest, most useless and plain uninteresting sections of Jersey', adding, 'he sort of catarrh-mumbles his ditties in a disgruntled mushmouth, sorta like Robbie Robertson on Quaaludes with Dylan barfing down the back of his neck.' Pretty harsh words, but Bangs does have something positive to say: 'What makes Bruce totally unique and cosmically surfeiting is his words. Hot damn, what a passel o'verbiage.'

In his *Village Voice* column, Robert Christgau had similarly mixed feelings. He believed 'the jokey lingo and absurdist energy … are exactly the excesses that made Dylan a genius instead of a talent.' Nevertheless, he believed numbers such as 'The Angel' and 'Mary Queen Of Arkansas' were 'turgid unaccompanied acoustic horrors that could scare anybody off this particular Dylan hype.'

Perhaps most enthusiastic was Peter Knobler, the editor of *Crawdaddy!* magazine: '[Springsteen] sings with a freshness and urgency I haven't heard since I was rocked by 'Like A Rolling Stone'.' But if there were some kind words from the critics, record buyers were less enthusiastic. The album peaked at number 60 in the US, and didn't initially chart at all in the UK, although 12 years later, some unexpected, if late, enthusiasm among British fans sent the album all the way to number 41.

'Blinded By The Light' (Springsteen)

'Blinded By The Light' is a kaleidoscope of images and ideas, and one way to make sense of it is to identify the characters we meet in the first verse of the song. In addition to the speaker/singer, there are the following individuals: 'madman drummers bummers and Indians in the summer'; 'the teenage diplomat'; 'the adolescent' pumping his way into his hat; 'some all-hot half-shot'; 'some fleshpot mascot'; 'young Scott with a slingshot' and his lover, whom he throws in the sand; and, finally, 'some bloodshot forget-me-not'.

It doesn't take long to figure out that these characters are, in large measure, created through the use of rhyme, which is apparent not only in their names but in their actions, as in the line: 'And some flesh*pot* ma*scot* was tied into a lover's *knot* with a what*not* in her hand'. Depending on how you like your lyrics, the way that Springsteen uses rhyme as something like a battering ram to keep 'Blinded By The Light' moving forward is either one of the central delights of the song, or its most annoying quality.

In his *Rolling Stone* interview, Jann Wenner remarks that 'rhyming 'mumps' with 'in the dumps' is really kind of cringey.' (And, of course, he might have given a couple of dozen other instances of comical rhymes in the song.) Springsteen responds: 'It was really youthful. I immediately started to move away from that [in *The Wild, The Innocent & The E Street Shuffle*] toward my soul influences.'

Youthful, though they may be, the rhymes in 'Blinded By The Light' are its heart and soul. Through them, Springsteen creates a surreal, carnival atmosphere. The activities in which the characters are engaged include, or appear to include, music-making, music-listening, dancing, masturbation, drug-taking, love-making, preaching, drinking and fighting. In short, it's just another wild Saturday night on the Jersey Shore.

The rat-a-tat of wordplay rides along on an incredibly catchy tune built on three major chords and the dominant's relative minor – in other words, the same pattern used in thousands of other pop songs. From the opening licks, Springsteen's electric guitar playing is funky and miles away from the acoustic songs that will follow, but what truly makes the song memorable is the saxophone work of Clarence Clemons. One of only two songs on the album on which he is featured, 'Blinded By The Light' finds him blowing his horn beneath, above, behind and in front of Springsteen's singing, so that the two engage in a kind of groovy duet throughout the song. Then, in the outro, Mad Dog Lopez's drumming joins in the fun, with singer, saxophonist and percussionist all doing their best to rise to the top of the mix as the song fades – the album is off to a terrific start.

In a perfect world, 'Blinded By The Light' would have been a radio hit, though maybe it was a bit too long and too loquacious. In February 1977, after sweetening the instrumentation and substantially trimming the lyrics and running time, Manfred Mann's Earth Band released a cover version of the song that went to the top of the charts in the US and to number six in the

UK, long after Springsteen had moved on to other sounds and styles. Interestingly, the rewritten line 'revved up like a deuce' was heard by many listeners (at the time, I was one of them) as 'revved up like a *douche*'. Springsteen's response: 'I have a feeling that's why the song rocketed up to number one.'

'Growin' Up' (Springsteen)

One of the strongest songs on *Asbury Park*, 'Growin' Up' makes use of some of the same rapid-fire rhyming, imagery and wordplay. The singer, for instance, claims he 'was open to pain and crossed by the rain/And I walked on a crooked crutch/I strolled all alone through a fallout zone/And came out with my soul untouched'.

Yet what might be called the logorrhea of 'Blinded By The Light' is more disciplined here, and the song is the better for it. According to the lyrics, for Springsteen, 'growin' up' basically consisted of thumbing his nose at the adult world whenever it tried to tell him what to do. The tag line leading into the chorus, which is basically just the title, is especially funny in the middle verse: 'When they said, 'Come down', I threw up'.

Indeed, the song is rife with moments where the singer is winking at us through his use of puns and hyperbole. In the second stanza, he 'pushed B-52 and bombed them with the blues', with B-52 representing, of course, both the B-52 Stratofortress bomber and the number on a jukebox corresponding to a record he's chosen to play. He extends this metaphor in the next line, singing: 'I broke all the rules, strafed my old high school/Never once gave thought to landing'.

In the third verse, one can't help but smile at his exaggerated claim that he 'took month-long vacations in the stratosphere/And you know it's really hard to hold your breath'. Physically impossible, yes, but to legions of stoned high school kids, the image surely rang true.

We've already encountered go-carts and side cars in 'Blinded By The Light', but the image toward the end of 'Growin' Up' sounds more like the automobile-obsessed Springsteen of *Born To Run* and *Darkness On The Edge Of Town*: 'I swear I found the key to the universe/In the engine of an old parked car'.

Musically, the song is a gem. Other than the variations on C that open each verse, 'Growin' Up' is basically just four chords, with a major seventh tossed into the chorus for good measure; still, it *sounds* like something much bigger is going on. The song begins with David Sancious playing some aching arpeggios on the piano. Springsteen begins singing, and soon we hear his acoustic guitars (twinned, one coming from each speaker), followed by Lopez's excited drumming. If Gary Tallent's bass often blends into the background, here it is foregrounded and punches the song forward. After the second chorus, Sancious delivers a rocking solo that segues into the opening figure on solo piano, over which Springsteen sings. Halfway through the verse, the guitars, drums and bass kick in again. The title is repeated, then the track quickly ends with just a few notes on the piano.

It's a great, compact song that tells a story just about any rebellious American teenager can relate to. Though it did not become a radio hit, 'Growin' Up' continues, decades later, to periodically appear in Springsteen's live repertoire, and it was the opening song in his theatrical hit, *Springsteen On Broadway*.

'Mary Queen Of Arkansas' (Springsteen)

Perhaps the most awkward song on the album is 'Mary Queen Of Arkansas'. Partly, that's because its narrative is so hard to pin down.

In 1971, the year before the song was written, there had been a big-budget production of *Mary Queen Of Scots*. Is Springsteen alluding ironically to the historical drama, transporting Mary from Scotland to Arkansas and re-casting himself as Queen Elizabeth? Even in the anything-goes world of *Asbury Park*, that seems unlikely.

Or is Mary Queen of Arkansas simply Mother Mary, that central figure from Springsteen's Catholic upbringing still hovering over his life and thought? That's a bit more probable. After all, in the opening stanza, 'the sky is grown with cloud seed sown/and a bastard's love can be redeeming'. Is the sky, and later 'the big top', which 'is for dreamers', a symbol for heaven? Is the bastard – i.e., the singer – Jesus? After all, the singer 'was not born to live to die', and neither was Jesus, who was resurrected after his earthly death. Possibly.

The most common explanation is that Mary is a transvestite or transexual. Some fan forums suggest Springsteen acknowledged as much in a concert in Pittsburgh in 2014, and there is a good deal to support a reading of Mary as transexual, particularly the lines 'You're not man enough for me to hate/Or woman enough for kissing'. Mary's less-than-traditionally feminine appearance is affirmed when the song refers to her 'soft hulk'. Similarly, the line that Mary waits 'to lie in bait' and almost has the singer 'believing' confirms that her appearance is, indeed, 'deceiving', possibly because she is cross-dressing. However, the claim that Mary 'was not born for queening' is ambiguous: does it mean she isn't really a drag queen, or that, because she was born a biological male, she is unable to fully inhabit the role of queen? Or is it something else altogether?

Obviously, the song inspires lots of basically unanswerable questions. The crazy jumble of images in the album's first two tracks works partly because the tempo of the songs matches the speed of Springsteen's delivery. However, when everything is decelerated to a torturous slowness, as on the third track, with Springsteen dragging out the words rather than rushing them, it becomes clear just how confusing the relationship is between Mary and the singer. They seem to inhabit a real or metaphorical circus, and yet three times we hear about the comings and goings of the 'the servants'. It's hard to imagine what these domestic attendants are doing in the run-down world of 'bastards' and 'acrobats', 'acid brats' and 'wharf rats'.

In *Magic In The Night*, Rob Kirkpatrick calls 'The Angel', a later song on *Asbury Park*, and 'Mary Queen of Arkansas' a couple of 'pretentious failures.' In *Born To Run: The Bruce Springsteen Story*, Dave Marsh is equally harsh. Describing the song's lyrics as 'cumbersome', he goes on to say that the track 'demands more focused writing' than Springsteen's style at the time can provide.

'Does This Bus Stop At 82nd Street?' (Springsteen)

Possibly because 'Does This Bus Stop At 82nd Street?', the shortest song on *Asbury Park*, comes right after the longest, it feels even shorter. At 2:05, it has the energy and structure of a punk song from a few years down the road, although The Ramones would never have come up with such a plethora of images and ideas, not to mention catchy rhymes.

Basically, the song – which Springsteen claimed in a 1975 interview with a Swedish disc jockey was actually written on the bus – describes the singer boarding a bus, presumably in New Jersey, and taking it into New York City. By now, the sort of characters the singer encounters, with their rhyming connections to one another, are familiar. We meet 'wizard imps and sweat sock pimps', along with 'interstellar mongrel nymphs', and Rex, whose 'lady left him limp'. 'Love's like that', Springsteen sings in an aside, 'sure it is'.

The band are in full throat for most of the song, with Tallent's bass rumbling in the pocket of Lopez's drumming. Springsteen makes the most out of his acoustic guitar, and Sancious's piano keeps the song upbeat.

Toward the end, Springsteen rolls out one of his first really great lines. When *The Daily News* asks 'Mary Lou' – another Mary, there will be so many of them in the Springsteen songbook! – 'for the dope', she simply replies: 'Man, the dope's that there's still hope'.

The next two lines, introducing us to a 'Señorita, Spanish rose', roll in at the same tempo, then suddenly things become slow and mournful as 'Uptown in Harlem, the señorita throws a rose to some lucky young matador'.

And then the song's over, almost, it feels before it has begun, though we've come on quite an expedition in 125 seconds, one that mimics the speed of the singer's impressions of journeying from small-town New Jersey into the metropolis.

'Lost In The Flood' (Springsteen)

The most ambitious and possibly the best song on *Asbury Park*, 'Lost In The Flood' closes out side one.

One main reason for the song's haunting quality is its spare arrangement. Springsteen sings but does not play guitar. Instead, Sancious's piano is the main instrument throughout, although he is joined by Tallent's bass and Lopez's drums. Sancious also plays the organ and the calliope – an instrument referenced in 'Blinded By The Light'. The calliope is associated with circuses and carnivals, and for Springsteen, its sound clearly calls up the 'boardwalk life' so essential to his early albums. The 'thunder' sound that opens the song is, famously, Steven Van Zandt, in his only appearance on the album, shaking Springsteen's Danelectro amplifier.

In *Glory Days*, Dave Marsh calls 'Lost In The Flood' 'as good a song as was written about Vietnam during the war.' Springsteen had actively campaigned to get a deferment from serving in the war, so it's not surprising that the song illustrates just how 'messed up' those returning from Vietnam were. In the opening line, we are introduced to 'the ragamuffin gunner', who is 'returning home like a hungry runaway'. As he 'walks through town all alone', he can hear the whispers of the high school girls saying, 'He must be from the fort'. It's a vivid picture of PTSD long before the term was popularized.

Then the camera pans out to the 'countryside', which is burning with 'wolfman fairies dressed in drag for homicide'. These persons, who seem to have both masculine ('wolfman') and feminine ('fairies') characteristics, are evidently wreaking havoc on everything, in particular the Catholic church, where they are 'breaking beams and crosses with a spastic's reeling perfection'. Indeed, the chaos that has been let loose extends all the way to Rome, where 'Nuns run bald through Vatican halls pleading immaculate conception'.

Somehow, in the next line, we find ourselves back on Main Street, where 'everybody's wrecked … from drinking unholy blood'. And then there's a new character, Sticker, smiling sweetly, while the ragamuffin gunner has reappeared, breathing deeply, 'his ankles caked in mud'. Then the singer inserts himself into his song, directly addressing 'Gunner Man', telling him that he's not stuck in mud, but rather in quicksand. 'Have you thrown your senses to the war?' he asks. 'Or did you lose them in the flood?'

Unlike the rhyme-overdrive of 'Blinded By The Light', there's a seriousness here, despite the cavalcade of surreal images. 'The flood' may be metaphorical, though clearly it gestures towards its Biblical precedent, yet it is just as sweeping as any actual deluge.

The second verse introduces us to a new character, or possibly a new incarnation of Gunner Man: 'That pure American brother, dull-eyed and empty faced'. His visage may not shine with intelligence, but he sure knows how to race cars, and to tell stories of his racing exploits: 'The kids call him Jimmy the Saint'. However, racing cars on a Jersey night is not enough for Jimmy, so, with his Chevy stock Super 8 decorated with 'red, white and blue flash paint', he 'rides headfirst into a hurricane and disappears into a point'. Still, despite his disappearance, he leaves behind a legend, 'a real highwayman's farewell'. Indeed, this verse adumbrates a whole line of guys in cars who are willing to risk their lives for the intoxicating thrill of power and speed as it is manifested in an American automobile.

The final verse takes us back into New York City, 'where Eighth Avenue sailors in satin shirts whisper in the air'. Mary Queen of Arkansas would be right at home here, in what appears to be a gay-friendly neighborhood.

However, the place is rife with danger. There's a shoot-out with the cops, and in the final chorus, we're confronted with the indifference the denizens of the song must feign in order to survive: 'Somebody said, 'Hey man, did you see that?/His body hit the street with such a beautiful thud''. It's a heartstopper of an ending, and when the singer asks us right afterwards if 'those poor cats' were 'lost in the flood', we must answer: 'Dude. Most definitely they were'.

'The Angel' (Springsteen)

'Mary Queen Of Arkansas' notwithstanding, the first side of *Greetings From Asbury Park, N.J.* has been largely successful, especially coming from an unknown kid from the Jersey Shore. It's a shame, therefore, that rather than capitalizing on side one's energy, the second side of the album begins with 'The Angel', the slowest song on the record. Again, David Sancious's piano is the central instrument, with jazzman Richard Davis bowing the double bass toward the end of the song. No drums, no guitar: this is a ballad, and a lethargic one, for sure.

Still, if 'The Angel' is often paired with 'Mary Queen Of Arkansas' to demonstrate what's worst about the album (it can be pretentious and boring), 'The Angel' is two minutes shorter and at least has a clear through-line. Moreover, like the second verse of 'Lost In The Flood', it points to some of the themes about young men and their machines that Springsteen will develop more fully on subsequent records.

Essentially, the song is about the Angel and his love for his motorcycle. While it's a dangerous vehicle, 'Poison oozing from his engine/Wielding love as a lethal weapon', he treats his bike like a lover, 'humpin' his hunk metal whore', and he clearly values it above all other things, including his fellow bikers (the 'hunch-backed children') and even the ingenue ('Madison Avenue's claim to fame/In a trainer bra with eyes like rain') who comes onto him at the end of the song.

While most of 'The Angel', even with its hyperbole, is fairly straightforward, the ending revives the surrealistic feel of earlier tracks. One minute, the girl is rubbing against the motorcycle's 'weather-beaten frame', asking 'the angel for his name', and just a few lines later, as she continues to stroke 'polished chrome', she is suddenly lying 'beside the angel's bones'.

Did the angel suddenly keel over, his flesh dissolving in fast-time like a corpse in a horror movie? Have years passed since he and the girl first met? Or is the whole thing just a metaphor, with 'the angel's bones' simply another way of describing him or his motorcycle? It's unclear, with the final sung note coinciding with the final note on the piano.

In 1974, speaking with Jerry Gilbert of the British rock magazine *ZigZag*, Springsteen claimed that "The Angel' was completed in 15 minutes, with the songwriter pronouncing, 'It's one of the most sophisticated things I've done.' Twenty-two years later, in another interview, he had a much different take: 'What the hell was I talking about in that song?'

'For You' (Springsteen)

Who is the 'you' in the title of this song? A number of fan forums suggest that the person addressed is Springsteen's girlfriend, Diane Lozito, who is also the subject of 'Rosalita (Come Out Tonight)' on *The Wild, The Innocent & The E Street Shuffle*, but there are no verified sources showing that Springsteen ever made this claim.

Whether or not 'you' is Lozito, another woman, or simply an amalgam of Springsteen's paramours, real and imagined, what is clear is that the person in the song is both dynamic and depressed. On the one hand, in the first verse, she seems confident, even dismissive: she doesn't even give the narrator time to cover his tracks; in the second verse, she is compared to superman, 'born with the power of a locomotive/Able to leap tall buildings in a single bound'; and in the third verse, her 'strength is devastating in the face of all these odds'.

At the same time, there are number of instances suggesting she is suffering from mental and physical exhaustion: her 'barroom eyes shine vacancy'; she has to crawl into the singer's ambulance because her 'pulse is getting weak'; she barely has 'the strength to speak'; even her surgeon 'says it's too late'; she was once 'broken on the beach'; and, of course, as we hear twice, her 'life was one long emergency'.

Indeed, what seems to be most strongly implied is that the woman either attempted or committed suicide. In fact, the third verse begins: 'And your Chelsea suicide with no apparent motive'. In the fourth verse, we learn that she 'left to find a better reason than the one we were living for'. If she is dead, the fact that Springsteen is singing directly to her could just mean that he is singing to her memory.

On the other hand, she may have survived all the trauma described in the song. After all, at the end of the final verse, Springsteen addresses her in the present, not the past, tense: 'And who am I to ask you to lick my sores?'

Regardless of the woman's fate, this is one of Springsteen's great character sketches, as detailed and nuanced as anything he would compose on later albums. The woman is so complex she 'could laugh and cry in a single sound', and so sensitive she could hear the 'metal-tempered engine on an alien, distant shore'.

The full band (minus Clemons), along with Springsteen's acoustic guitar, ensure that the energy necessary to convey the subject's vitality is present throughout the song. Lopez's drumming is varied and sensitive, and Tallent's bass is surprisingly funky. Sancious plays piano throughout, but he inserts an organ during the first chorus, and for the rest of the song, it adds color and texture to the tuneful music of this memorable track.

'Spirit In The Night' (Springsteen)

Writing in the *New Musical Express* in 1975, Andrew Tyler describes the song as one of Springsteen's 'few genuinely stirring melodies, even though it leans too heavily on Van Morrison.' Springsteen, a big fan of the Irish singer-songwriter, might well have taken this criticism as a compliment.

In an interview with Ed Sciaky of Philadelphia's WMMR radio station in 1974, Springsteen said, 'For some reason I always imagined Joe Cocker doing 'Spirit In The Night'. When I wrote the song, I had his kind of voice in mind, which is something that I rarely do.'

Manfred Mann's Earth Band certainly envisioned the song as performed by someone else – themselves. Their version reached number 40 in the US. Other artists have recorded the song, but 'Spirit In The Night' has become a staple of Springsteen's live shows for decades, and for good reason. As with 'Blinded By The Light', 'Spirit In The Night' is not limited to a few solos by Clarence Clemons. Instead, from the opening note, his saxophone is omnipresent and the most memorable musical aspect of the song.

Interestingly, Tallent and Sancious had another commitment on the day 'Spirit In The Night' was recorded, so it was Springsteen playing a rough barroom piano, with studio musician Harold Wheeler brought in afterwards to add some professional touches on the keys. Springsteen also plays bass – not with as much authority as Tallent, but he certainly knows the rhythm of his own song. There's also a bit of groovy, almost beatnik syncopation from the handclapping of Springsteen, Clemons and Lopez.

Despite the wild names of the characters – Crazy Janey and Mission Man (the narrator), Wild Billy and G-man, Hazy Davy and Killer Joe – the action described in the song, basically some teenage kids driving out to the local lake to party, is one with which millions of Americans would be familiar. As Dave Marsh points out in *Born To Run: The Bruce Springsteen Story, Volume 1*, 'One understands Greasy Lake as an archetype of similar places the listener has known, just as one understands the characters to be universal variations of figures in real life.'

Still, there are some interesting personal parallels, some of which have been confirmed by Springsteen himself. Hazy Davy is likely Springsteen's high school friend David Hazlett, although Springsteen has also said he was inspired by a character in The Band's 1971 song 'Moon Struck One'. Most prominently, Crazy Janey may be a stand-in for Diane Lozito of 'Rosalita' fame, while Wild Billy is likely Billy Cahill, a law student who was given that nickname because, in Lozito's words, he was a 'major party boy'. Springsteen famously stole Lozito away from Cahill for a while, but, in the end, her parents advised her to stick with the aspiring lawyer rather than the aspiring musician. (More about this relationship in 'Rosalita (Come Out Tonight)'.)

The climax of the story occurs in the muted bacchanal after Wild Billy distributes the 'dust out of his coonskin cap', which will 'show you where you're at', and the group arrives at Greasy Lake. There, the narrator and Janey make love in the dirt, while Killer Joe is passed out on the lawn, and the relationship between Wild Billy and Hazy Davy turns homoerotic as they dance in the moonlight to 'a soul fairy band'. Something happens, though, and 'Hazy Davy got really hurt:/He ran into the lake in just his socks and his shirt'.

Nevertheless, this madcap magical night seems to exist almost in the realm of a fairytale, for all Janey and her Mission Man need to do to leave it is to close their eyes, and then together they will move 'like spirits in the night, all night'.

Some fans have suggested that 'Crazy Janey' was inspired by a series of poems by the Irish poet W. B. Yeats about 'Crazy Jane'. Considering his youthful distaste for traditional education, that seems unlikely, although the influence has worked in the opposite direction, with American fiction writer T. C. Boyle taking the title for his story 'Greasy Lake' from 'Spirit In The Night'. In a 2000 letter to the *New York Times*, Boyle acknowledged that he had borrowed the name from Springsteen's song, but pointed out that he'd decided to go in a much darker direction in his story about teenagers driving down to a lake at night: 'a free take on [the song's] glorious spirit.'

'It's Hard To Be A Saint In The City' (Springsteen)
In his autobiography, Springsteen recalls that when he auditioned for John Hammond, he later learned that the producer was 'poised and ready to hate us', but when Hammond asked for a song, Springsteen played him 'It's Hard To Be A Saint In The City': 'When I was done, I looked up. That smile was still there, and I heard him say, 'You've got to be on Columbia Records.' One song – that's all it took.'

The recorded version of the song begins with Springsteen strumming his acoustic guitar while Lopez taps on the hi-hat. Soon, Sancious enters with a rollicking piano figure, but with Springsteen still slowly strumming and the hi-hat being the only sound from the drums, it almost sounds like the band is warming up. Then, as Tallent joins in on bass, Springsteen begins singing one of the liveliest songs on the album.

'It's Hard To Be A Saint In The City' is also very much in the tradition of boasting songs. The singer isn't exactly 'The Wild Rover' of Irish folk music, but he's something close. He tells us in the opening lines that he has 'skin like leather and the diamond-hard look of a cobra'. Among the other superlatives he lays on himself in the first two verses are that he bursts 'like a supernova', walks 'like Brando' and dances 'just like a Casanova'. He is the 'king of the alley' and 'prince of the paupers' and 'the pimp's main prophet'. Even the Southside Sisters admire him: 'Don't that man look pretty?'

And yet, it's not hard to see that some of this bragging is covering up for insecurities. After all, his luck is that of a 'backstreet gambler', and when things get tense and the devil appears, the singer is forced to dive 'into the heat', where, presumably, things will not go especially well for him.

The second variation on the title is sung by itself, without the rest of the chorus, and then the piano-driven bridge breaks up the four-chord pattern of the rest of the song as we move from the singer's bragging to a depiction of 'sages on the subway' who 'sit just like the living dead'. The chorus hits us with its quadruple rhymes of 'pretty', 'pity', 'gritty' and 'city' – an appropriate summation of the song's themes.

At a little over 16 minutes long, the second side of *Asbury Park* could have easily handled one more song, but perhaps it's best that Springsteen, Appel and company eschewed another sluggish ballad and ended instead on such a strong track. There would be plenty of time to extend his explorations of New York and the Jersey Shore in his next album, released that very same year.

The Wild, The Innocent And The E Street Shuffle (1973)

Personnel:

Bruce Springsteen: lead vocals, guitar, maracas on 'The E Street Shuffle', recorder on '4th Of July, Asbury Park (Sandy)', harmonica on 'Wild Billy's Circus Story', mandolin on 'Wild Billy's Circus Story'

Clarence Clemons: tenor saxophone (except 'Wild Billy's Circus Story'), backing vocals (except 'Wild Billy's Circus Story')

Danny Federici: backing vocals (except 'Wild Billy's Circus Story' and 'Incident On 57th Street'), accordion on '4th Of July, Asbury Park (Sandy)' and 'Wild Billy's Circus Story', organ on 'Kitty's Back', second piano on 'Incident On 57th Street'

Garry Tallent: bass guitar (except 'The E Street Shuffle' and 'Wild Billy's Circus Story'), tuba on 'The E Street Shuffle' and 'Wild Billy's Circus Story', backing vocals on 'Kitty's Back'

David Sancious: piano (except 'The E Street Shuffle' and 'Wild Billy's Circus Story'), organ, clavinet on 'The E Street Shuffle', soprano saxophone on 'The E Street Shuffle', electric piano on 'The E Street Shuffle', backing vocals on 'New York City Serenade', organ solo on 'Kitty's Back', Mellotron on 'New York City Serenade', string arrangement on 'New York City Serenade'

Vini 'Mad Dog' Lopez: drums, percussion, backing vocals on 'The E Street Shuffle', 'Kitty's Back' and 'New York City Serenade', cornet on 'The E Street Shuffle'

Richard Blackwell: percussion on 'The E Street Shuffle' and 'New York City Serenade'

Albany 'Al' Tellone: baritone saxophone on 'The E Street Shuffle'

Suki Lahav: choir vocals on '4th Of July, Asbury Park (Sandy)' and 'Incident On 57th Street'

Recorded at 914 Sound Studios, Blauvelt, New York, between 14 May and 23 September 1973

Producers: Mike Appel and Jim Cretecos

Release date: 5 November 1973

Running time: 46:43

Label: Columbia

Album charts: US: 59, UK: 33 (1985)

Eleven months after the release of *Greetings From Asbury Park, N.J.*, in November 1973, Springsteen rolled out his second album, *The Wild, The Innocent & The E Street Shuffle*, the title nodding to a cheesy 1959 Western: *The Wild And The Innocent*. 'On the second album,' he says in Dave Marsh's book *Two Hearts*, 'I started slowly to find out who I am and where I wanted to be.' That person was emphatically not the solo acoustic singer-songwriter of 'Mary Queen Of Arkansas', but instead the leader of a big and dexterous rock and soul band capable of hard-driving songs like the title track and opuses like the closer, 'New York City Serenade'.

Writing in *Melody Maker* in 1974, Robert Hilburn argued that the album 'made enormous strides towards giving Springsteen [a] separate identity' from singer-songwriter acts like John, Prine, Jackson Browne and Loudoun Wainwright III. 'Without sacrificing the surrealistic lyrics, both his themes – normally reflecting the innocence, wonder, frustrations, urgency of youth – were more disciplined and his musical backing bolder than in the first album.'

Whereas *Asbury Park* sometimes felt like a folk album with rock 'n' roll grafted onto it, on *The Wild, The Innocent & The E Street Shuffle,* Springsteen embraces the band itself as an essential element of his compositions. Critic Matt Mitchell reckons that Springsteen and his band played 210 shows in 1973, during the time when his second album was being composed and recorded, and you can hear that tightness in the band, the way they bring out every nuance of a song while simultaneously rocking as hard as the song requires.

Lyrically, there are still great runs of verbosity, with the rhyming dictionary firmly in hand and the verses overwhelming the choruses. And the songs continue to regale us with the exploits of characters with memorable names like Power 13, Jack Knife and Diamond Jackie. But on the second album, Springsteen doesn't seem to be quite so desperate to cram as many words in a track as possible. Instead, he gives the melodies and the crack playing of his ensemble some room to work outside his singing.

In fact, Springsteen's second album is probably his most musically adventurous. There are horns aplenty and a lovely string arrangement by Sancious on 'New York City Serenade'. Sancious may, indeed, be the unsung hero of the album: he adds clavinet, Mellotron, electric piano and soprano sax, and his piano playing was never better. Other instruments not normally found on a rock 'n' roll album, like Danny Federici's accordion and Gary Tallent's tuba, add delight and surprise (although more of the latter with the tuba). It's a musical stew that nearly always works, and even when it doesn't quite gel, as on 'Wild Billy's Circus Story', there are still passages a listener can admire for their daring.

The front cover, with Springsteen's name and the title at the top in a thin white font, is a close-up of the boss, looking mysterious and sexy. His right forefinger touches his lip and brushes his scraggly black beard as he stares off into the distance, with his haunted, hooded eyes, thinking deep thoughts.

In his book (written with Don Reo) *Big Man: Real Life & Tall Tales*, Clarence Clemons describes the 1973 photograph taken by David Garb for the back of the album jacket: 'We had been surfing that day. We knew we had this photo shoot, so we wanted to go inside and change. But Dave said, 'No, you look great like this', so we ended up taking those pictures, and then we went back out surfing. You can feel the summer when you look at that picture. You can feel the Jersey Shore.' They look very relaxed, indeed. Clarence 'Nick' Clemons and Vini 'Mad Dog' Lopez wear shorts and open shirts. Springsteen is very tanned in a green wifebeater, Sancious and a long-haired and bearded

Gary W. Tallent are shoeless (well, Tallent has one shoe off). Only Danny Federici sports a shirt, pants and shoes. They're at the Shore, after all.

Robert Christgau, the master of the backhanded compliment, opined in his *Consumer Guide* review: 'Folkie trappings behind him, Springsteen has created a funky, vivacious rock 'n' roll that's too eager and zany ever to be labeled tight, suggesting jazz heard through an open window with one R&B saxophone, or Latin music out in the street with zero conga drums.'

However, *Rolling Stone* was a supporter of Springsteen's right from the start, and Ken Emerson raved about the new record. Acknowledging that *Greetings From Asbury Park* 'sounded like 'Subterranean Homesick Blues' played at 78, a typical five-minute track bursting with more words than this review', Emerson argued that the songs on the new album were 'longer, more ambitious and more romantic; and yet, wonderfully, they lose little of *Greetings*' rollicking rush'.

Unfortunately, by the time the album was ready for release, Springsteen's two great champions at Columbia, John Hammond and Clive Davis, had left the building. The new suits were not impressed. Perversely, Springsteen writes in *Born To Run*, Columbia's A&R men were even asking radio stations to take his songs out of rotation because they were 'too long'. Not surprisingly, as with the first album, initial sales were mediocre. More than a decade later, sales picked up, especially in Britain, when Springsteen toured with *Born In The U.S.A.*, but back when the album was released, it took a year and a half to struggle up to the number 59 spot in the US, and it did not chart at all in the UK.

Luckily, the band's constant touring put Springsteen in touch with influential DJs throughout the country, who provided 'much love and valuable support and a well-needed home for us and our music.' The groundwork, at least, was there when *Born To Run* dropped two years later.

Even with the band having been a fixture of the concert circuit, all was not well within its ranks. In his autobiography, Springsteen says that during the recording of *The Wild, The Innocent & The E Street Shuffle*, 'one thing became clear: we needed a steadier hand at the drums. Vini was a beautiful drummer in his own wigged-out way. He was all about his own style.' However, the sound of the band was, and always would be, dictated by the Boss himself. If Lopez's drumming was 'hyperactive', so was the man. His tendency to 'go completely postal within seconds' ultimately led to a fight with Clemons, and choosing between the two was a no-brainer for Springsteen. The Big Man would always win, and Springsteen wanted 'someone with a more sophisticated palate, with clearer and better time'. In 1974, Mad Dog was out of the band, eventually to be replaced by South Orange, New Jersey, native Max Weinberg.

'The E Street Shuffle' (Springsteen)

The opening song begins with a cacophony of horns: Clarence Clemons on the tenor saxophone, David Sancious on the soprano sax, Al Tellone on the baritone sax, bassist Gary Tallent on the tuba (who knew!) and drummer Vini Lopez on the cornet. They each blow their own thing for a couple of moments, then get in tune on a seven-note run accented at the end by the tuba. Then the horns die down as Springsteen plays one of the funkiest guitar riffs of his career.

The story told in the lyrics is, by now, a familiar one. A group of urban youths are hanging out at night, looking for something to do. The boys are cool 'prophets' who make 'all the little girls' souls grow weak'. The dudes are 'dressed in snakeskin suits packed with Detroit muscle', while their love interests are 'teenage tramps in skintight pants'.

In the second verse, we meet Power 13, fresh from giving 'a trooper all he had in a summer scuffle'. Fortunately, Power's girl, Little Angel, 'has been on the corner keeping those crazy boys out of trouble', though, like everyone, she can't resist the E Street Shuffle. Indeed, the brief bridge consists of Angel calling out, twice, 'Oh oh oh oh oh, everybody form a line!'

In the third stanza, the 'boy prophets' join Little Angel at Easy Joe's, where the dancing continues, and 'them sweet summer nights turn into summer dreams', with 'summer' being the keyword not only in this song but throughout *The Wild, The Innocent & The E Street Shuffle*. Indeed, critic Matt Mitchell speculates that this 'summer album' is 'maybe the greatest one ever written'.

After three minutes of joyous, rapid-fire singing, Springsteen gives the band a chance to play for a half-minute. It's horns and a guitar solo and lots of shouting from the floor so that we feel as though we're in the midst of a party just this side of out-of-control.

Then, at 3:35, there's a false ending, followed immediately by the funky guitar riff, then keyboards, bass and drums and a horn riff that goes into a long fade, as we imagine all those kids E Street Shuffling into the vanishing point.

'4th Of July, Asbury Park (Sandy)' (Springsteen)

'Sandy', Springsteen writes in *Born To Run*, 'was a composite of some of the girls I'd known along the Shore. I used the boardwalk and the closing down of the town as a metaphor for the end of a summer romance and the changes I was experiencing in my own life.' He also notes that at the time he was writing the song, he was living over a garage with a funny, Italian 'beatific tomboy, with just the hint of a lazy eye' who 'wore a pair of glasses that made me think of the wonders of the library.' That paradoxical sense that the subject of the song is both a very specific person *and* an amalgam of many other young women gives the song its haunting quality in the way that every heartthrob, and every heartache, feels both maddeningly particular and yet truly universal.

It's not hard to see why this song quickly became a fan favorite and a staple of Springsteen's live shows. First, there is the enigmatic and appealing Sandy, who is both the subject of the singer's advances – 'O love me tonight, for I may never see you again' – and of his warnings: 'For me this boardwalk life's through, babe./You ought to quit this scene too'. And yet, despite the ambivalence that hovers over their relationship, each time Springsteen sings the hook – 'Sandy girl', followed by 'my my' or 'na na na' or 'sha la la, baby' – we can feel his desire for her.

'4th Of July, Asbury Park' is one of the Boss's most carefully wrought lyrics, with many of the lines approaching the quality of literature. Take the opening two lines, for instance – 'Sandy, the fireworks are hailing over Little Eden tonight,/Forcing a light into all those stony faces left stranded on this warm July'. There's the unusual but perfect verb phrase to describe the fireworks ('are hailing'), the specificity of place ('Little Eden') and the close observation of the way the exploding fireworks look on the 'stony faces' of the people who are 'left stranded' – what an inventive way to describe people on a beach on Independence Day!

And that's not even to mention the description of the boardwalk characters: the 'switchblade lovers', 'the wizards … down on Pinball Way', the boys from the casino 'with their shirts open like Latin lovers' and the respectful (for the time) depiction of transpeople: 'Them boys in their high heels, ah, Sandy,/ Their skins are so white'. In the final verse, when the singer describes the waitress who lost her desire for him, he speaks of her wistfully rather than with bitterness. Like him, she's just one more casualty of the boardwalk, as is Madame Marie (an actual Jersey Shore palm and tarot card reader), who is busted by the cops 'For telling fortunes better than they do'.

Then there's the music, led by Danny Federici's romantic accordion playing – he could have had a great second gig strolling through Italian restaurants – and bolstered by Springsteen's moody, delicate acoustic guitar and Tallent's evocative basslines. This is a song you can imagine being played on the jukebox of a Jersey Shore dive, one where temporary lovers sway in each other's arms as the smell of cologne and perfume, sweat and cigarette smoke, and a salty hint of ocean waves permeates the room.

By the time the third and final chorus rolls around, and the singer claims, 'Oh, love me tonight, and I promise I'll love you forever', adding, 'Oh, I mean it Sandy girl', we can be pretty sure that neither he nor Sandy believes that empty promise – though whether or not she accepts his invitation is an open question. Whatever happens between the two on the night in question, the next day is bound to be one of disappointment, but perhaps tinged with a touch of poignancy.

'Kitty's Back' (Springsteen)

In his autobiography, Springsteen writes: "Kitty's Back' was a remnant of some of the jazz-tinged rock I occasionally played with a few of my earlier bands.' He adds: 'Just when you thought the song was over, you'd be surprised by another section, taking the music higher. It was, in spirit, what I'd taken from the finales of the great soul revues.'

The song was a live favorite early in Springsteen's career, and it's easy to see why. 'Kitty's Back' begins with a blistering, bluesy lead guitar that lasts nearly a minute. The solo is accompanied by saxophone, Danny Federici's organ and Springsteen's double-tracked guitar, which gives the 'horn section', i.e., Clemons, a much fuller sound than if he were playing alone. The singing, as numerous critics and fans have pointed out, is almost incidental to the many changes the song goes through, offering individual members of the band their moment to shine.

The sax/organ/guitar ensemble reappears in full after the second verse. Then Sancious himself takes a turn at the organ that quickly gives way to a second Springsteen multi-tracked guitar solo. The 'horns' argue with the guitar for a while before they give up the fight, and Sancious is back at the organ for another solo, which is soon joined by the rest of the band, Clemons leading the way. Compared to his output so far, it's an awfully long time for Springsteen to go without singing, although when listening to *Steel Mill Band*, the live recordings of Springsteen, Federici, Lopez and Steven Van Zandt from 1970, Springsteen's roots as a jam band leader make it clear that 'Kitty's Back' isn't an entirely new direction for him.

There's a third verse, after which Springsteen advises the protagonist, his audience and himself to 'Get tight, get right'. The song slows down, the organ all unhurried and churchy, then the band whisper eight times, 'Here she comes', and we finally get something like a chorus, eight iterations of 'Kitty's back in town', followed by either 'Oh-oh-oh all right' or 'Here she comes now'. A late bridge is followed by the protagonist moaning 'Ooh, what can I do?' and then the band singing 'Ooh-ooh-ooh-ooh alright, oh, alright' until Clemons's tenor saxophone rises up and takes the song to its conclusion.

As to the lyrics, are they the silliest in Springsteen's oeuvre? Quite possibly. The story is simple: A gentleman named Catlong has lost his girl, Kitty, to a fellow named Big Pretty, but now she's back in town and he can't stop thinking about her. There are some rather bad cat jokes – Big Pretty is a 'top cat', Kitty is 'down in the city pound' – along with some of the urban scene-setting we've become accustomed to, but ultimately, the song is basically, as Springsteen said in a 1975 interview with a European journalist, 'a strip tease number … It's a strange song. Sort of big band-y. I like it because it communicates the heat.'

'Wild Billy's Circus Story' (Springsteen)

Any popular song that begins with someone – Tallent, in this case – puffing on a tuba is in for an uphill ride, and 'Wild Billy's Circus Story' is a track that often separates the Boss's true believers from merely devoted fans. It does repay repeated listenings, but it's hard not to tag 'Wild Billy's Circus Story' as the weakest song on the album.

Tallent on tuba is soon joined by Springsteen on acoustic guitar and Federici on the accordion. Then the accompanying instruments fade, and it's just Springsteen and his guitar telling another story about the eclectic characters on the Jersey Shore, though in this case, they are all circus folk.

For 1973, this is a relatively sympathetic portrayal of characters who were often derided by the straight world as freaks, but we may flinch a bit as we meet 'Fat lady, big mama, Missy Bimbo' and 'the man-beast' and 'the midget'. Nevertheless, throughout the song, they show themselves to be a tight-knit group who mostly have each other's backs.

The song is flavored by a whirlwind of instrumentation. Halfway through the second verse, Springsteen joins himself on the mandolin, then the tuba is back with its insistent single note for verse three. The tuba drops out for some fluttery notes on the accordion in a short pre-bridge that concludes with a drum roll. Then, in the bridge, the steady rhythm starts to go awry, becoming something not too far from an art song with a baleful keyboard backing. However, just when the song seems about to spin out of control, the rhythm, led by the acoustic guitar, catches the spirit of the first part of the song, though only for a moment, for soon an overdubbed Springsteen is blowing on his harmonica and the accordion is back, along with a dash of saxophone to accompany the elephants as they 'dance real funky'.

The final verse, initially accompanied by the mandolin, then just the acoustic guitar, winds down with the ringmaster asking a boy if he wants to accompany the circus on their next stop to Nebraska. We never hear the boy's reply, as the song ends on a blast of guitar, tuba and accordion.

Springsteen calls the song 'a black comedy based on my memories of the fairs and the Clyde Beatty-Cole Circus that visited Freehold every summer when I was a kid.' And, yes, it is that, but in the midst of an ambitious rock and soul album, where even the slow numbers have a definite forward momentum, 'Wild Billy's Circus Story' feels musically and lyrically like something of a backwater eddy.

'Incident On 57th Street' (Springsteen)

'Incident On 57th Street', the first song on side two, begins with a lovely piano figure played by Sancious. He's soon joined by Federici on the organ and a couple of echoey guitar runs before Springsteen dives into a brief solo that leads to the introduction of the song's hero: Spanish Johnny. After his emergence from 'the underworld' – more likely the Holland Tunnel out of Jersey City than Hades itself – Spanish Johnny immediately finds himself in trouble. He tries to sell 'his heart to the hard girls over on Easy Street', but they know 'hearts are cheap these days', and soon their pimps are beating on Johnny with axes, calling him a cheater and a liar.

Fortunately for him, 'out of the shadows' comes a girl's voice, and Johnny is rescued by Puerto Rican Jane. The couple are soon off to a bar where the 'singer was singing something about going home'.

The passage of time is hazy in the song, but by the next verse, the two seem to have been together for a while when Johnny discovers 'the cops have found the vein'. It's an interesting image, almost as if the police have tapped into the very source that carries the city's heroin into the myriad bloodstreams of its users. In any case, after many outlaw denizens of the city have abandoned their switchblades and fled for 'the woods', we see Johnny 'sitting on the fire escape/Watching the kids playing down the street'.

Unlike many early Springsteen songs, where there are so many characters and events that it is sometimes difficult to tell who the protagonist is, in 'Incident on 57th Street', Johnny and Jane are clearly the hero and heroine of the story. Indeed, with Spanish Johnny looking 'like a cool Romeo' and Puerto Rican Jane restyled as 'a late Juliet', it's not surprising that a number of critics have compared the song to Shakespeare's *Romeo And Juliet* and Leonard Bernstein's *West Side Story*, although Springsteen claimed at the time not to have read the play or seen the musical.

Before the three iterations of the chorus at the end, 'those romantic young boys' who have appeared throughout the song present a temptation to Johnny that could well derail his relationship with Jane: 'You want to make a little easy money tonight?' they ask. The promise of picking up some fast cash in return for a supposedly small favor is one that Springsteen will return to in 'Meeting Across The River' on *Born To Run*, 'Atlantic City' on *Nebraska* and 'Easy Money' on *Wrecking Ball*. Making a big, stress-free score is the pipedream of small-time hoods everywhere, and in that regard, Spanish Johnny could be anyone with a chip on his shoulder and an impossible dream, one that always ends as a nightmare.

If the song concludes on a note of forlorn ambiguity, that's not surprising. In a 1975 radio interview, Springsteen said of 'Incident On 57th Street', along with several other songs: 'They're all about the same thing: decisions, escapes, the way various people cope with them. There are never any solutions, there are never any answers, because there are never any in real life.'

All along, the song is borne aloft by the superb musicianship of the band. Gary Tallent's bass is especially important in establishing a rhythm, while Sancious and Federici both play piano, with Sancious adding organ at key moments. Clemons is absent from the track, but Suki Lahav, wife of engineer Louis Lahav, makes up for his absence with some stellar vocals. Through the magic of overdubbing, she essentially becomes a one-woman choir. Interestingly, Suki later played violin with the E Street Band, but according to Mike Appel in Marc Eliot's *Thunder Road*, she and her husband moved back to Israel to save their marriage – she was falling in love with the Boss and he with her.

'Rosalita (Come Out Tonight)' (Springsteen)

The moment the last piano note of 'Incident On 57th Street' ends, 'Rosalita (Come Out Tonight)' begins, as though Springsteen couldn't wait to get started with what would become one of his most popular songs. It's a rocker, and rightly a fan favorite, one that closed many a Springsteen concert over the years.

The song tells a great story, and it does so accompanied by the most consistently upbeat music on the album. Springsteen pointed to the horn charts of Van Morrison as an inspiration, and you can certainly hear that in Clemons's saxophone playing, including his famous solo, which perfectly captures every mood of the song. Lopez's drumming alternately swings and rocks, and Sancious's organ and piano infuse the song with a rapturous spirit.

In *Songs*, Springsteen said of 'Rosalita (Come Out Tonight)': 'It was my 'getting out of town' preview for *Born To Run*, with more humor. I wrote it as a kiss-off to everybody who counted you out, put you down, or decided you weren't good enough.' And who was the girl whose parents were so against Springsteen? Interviewed in a 2024 French documentary entitled *Citizen Bruce: The American Pal*, Diane Lozito, purportedly the subject of *Asbury Park*'s 'For You', discussed what had been widely stated, that the song was based on Springsteen's courtship of her and her parents rejection of him because, in the words of Lozito's father: 'Musicians don't earn enough money and are tramps.' Still, Springsteen retained fond memories of Lozito decades afterwards, describing her in his memoir as 'a sweet blonde who I believe was the first gal I had successful intercourse with (though, due to the fog of war, I can't be absolutely sure).'

The song resulting from this autobiographical incident is a distant descendant of Robert Herrick's 'Corinna's Going A-Maying', in which the speaker advises his beloved to 'Rise and put on your foliage, and be seen/To come forth, like the spring-time, fresh and green'. Of course, Springsteen wouldn't be alluding to a poem he's unlikely to have known, but the 'stone desire' the singer has for Rosalita is very much in keeping with Herrick's 'proclamation made for May': love-making.

And what a pitch the singer makes to Rosalita! They are going to have so much fun, making 'that highway run', hanging out with friends like Jack the Rabbit and Weak Knee Willie and Sloppy Sue, playing pool and skipping school; they're going to 'Act real cool, stay out all night, it's gonna feel all right'.

Nevertheless, Rosalita's parents are firmly against her paramour, to the extent that her 'papa lowered the boom, he locked you in your room'. But in the penultimate verse, Springsteen has an ace up his sleeve: he reveals to Rosie's father that this is his 'last chance to get his daughter in a fine romance' because the record company just gave him 'a big advance'. There's a bit of bravado in that line. Springsteen's two underperforming albums, neither of which had produced a successful single, were hardly cause for 'a big advance' from Columbia. But, of course, Springsteen, who until recently was one of those rare artists who owned the rights to all their songs, got the last laugh, as usual. In 2021, he sold his entire catalog to Sony Music Entertainment for $550 million. A big advance, indeed.

The final verse offers more promises of good times, including hanging out in 'a pretty little place in Southern California, down San Diego way' where 'they play guitars all night and all day'. But will Rosie actually escape from her parents' clutches (how old is she, anyway?) and finally come sit by the fire of the Boss? As Rob Kirkpatrick writes in *Magic In The Night*, when Springsteen, at the end of the song, 'lets loose … a primal rock scream that is so triumphant, one senses that it almost doesn't matter if Rosie goes with him.'

'New York City Serenade' (Springsteen)
In classical music, a serenade, as its root suggests, is generally a light, calm, *serene* piece of music, typically to honor a person or event. For a Springsteen song, 'New York City Serenade' is, in fact, fairly serene, although there is one passage in the middle when the nearly ten-minute composition briefly shifts tone and rhythm.

It all begins with David Sancious scraping his piano strings – it *almost* sounds like a dulcimer – before he launches into a beautiful piano introduction. There's a little Rachmaninoff and some Gershwin, but whatever Sancious's inspirations were, musically this is far beyond Springsteen's compositional capabilities at the time. The Boss was always keen to take credit for his songwriting, but surely in this instance, Sancious deserves a co-writing nod.

After the first verse, notable for Springsteen's delicate acoustic guitar and Richard Blackwell's surprisingly effective congas, Sancious adds another crucial component of the song, a string arrangement he wrote and conducted. On Backstreets.com, Sancious recalls: 'I think the producer or the engineer found these three guys, these three violinists, who were music school teachers. They were from the local area. So the whole 'string section' was actually three people who got overdubbed … They go in, they rewind the song, they play it again, now it sounds larger and you just keep doing that.' Whatever method was used to get the strings on record, they add immeasurably to the sweep and majesty of the music.

For an early Springsteen number, especially one this long, the lyrics are remarkably terse. There is some repetition of lines, like 'No, she won't take the train', in reference to the woman in the 'handclap section' who's 'afraid them tracks are going to slow her down', and a call and response with the background vocalists – Clemons, Federici, Tallent and Lopez – toward the end of the song. However, the story itself doesn't differ much from those we've heard in previous songs. A group of local heroes/losers are hanging around the city after dark, looking for something worthwhile to do and getting the blues instead.

There are a couple of striking lines, evoking the place and mood of the song – 'This is midnight in Manhattan: this is no time to get cute' and 'Hey jazz man, oh play me your serenade,/Any deeper blue and you're playing in your grave' – but Springsteen's singing is often soft or whispered, which suits the mood of the song perfectly.

About halfway in, Clemons joins the party, his saxophone echoing in the background until the final two minutes, when he begins to blow for real. And though he's competing against the strings and Springsteen's ad-libbing, it's the sax that you remember as the serenade slowly wends towards its quiet conclusion.

Robert Christgau called 'New York City Serenade' 'as bathetic as you might fear', but that's an unfairly harsh assessment from a critic who has doled out his share of them. Granted, the final few minutes might have been clipped, but the song is a bold statement of Springsteen's ambition and a fitting conclusion to an album that has aged well in the more than 50 years since it was recorded.

Born To Run (1975)

Personnel:

Bruce Springsteen: vocals, guitar (except 'Meeting Across The River'), harmonica ('Thunder Road'), horn arrangement ('Tenth Avenue Freeze Out')

Roy Bittan: piano (except 'Born To Run'), organ ('Backstreets', 'She's The One' and 'Jungleland'), glockenspiel ('Thunder Road' and 'Night'), harpsichord ('Night' and 'She's The One'), backing vocals ('Thunder Road')

Clarence Clemons: saxophones (except 'Backstreets' and 'Meeting Across The River')

Garry Tallent: bass guitar (except 'Meeting Across The River')

Max Weinberg: drums (except 'Born To Run' and 'Meeting Across The River')

Ernest Carter: drums ('Born To Run')

Danny Federici: organ ('Born To Run'), glockenspiel ('Born To Run')

David Sancious: piano ('Born To Run'), Fender Rhodes piano ('Born To Run'), synthesizer ('Born To Run')

Mike Appel: backing vocals ('Thunder Road')

Steven Van Zandt: backing vocals ('Thunder Road'), horn arrangement ('Tenth Avenue Freeze-Out')

Randy Brecker: trumpet ('Tenth Avenue Freeze-Out' and 'Meeting Across The River'), flugelhorn ('Tenth Avenue Freeze-Out')

Michael Brecker: tenor saxophone ('Tenth Avenue Freeze-Out')

David Sanborn: baritone saxophone ('Tenth Avenue Freeze-Out')

Wayne Andre: trombone ('Tenth Avenue Freeze-Out')

Richard Davis: double bass ('Meeting Across The River')

Suki Lahav: violin ('Jungleland')

Charles Calello: string arrangements and conductor ('Jungleland')

Recorded at 914, Blauvelt, New York; Record Plant, New York City, between January 1974 and July 1975

Producers: Bruce Springsteen, Mike Appel, Jon Landau

Release date: 25 August 1975

Running time: 39:23

Label: Columbia

Album charts: US: 3; UK: 17

Singles charts: 'Born To Run' (US: 23, UK: 56); 'Tenth Avenue Freeze-Out' (US: 83)

In the opinion of its many fans, *Born To Run* is the greatest rock 'n' roll album ever recorded. That's a claim only true Springsteen fanatics would make for his first two albums. How did an eclectic rocker popular primarily in the Mid-Atlantic and Northeastern United States become a national and then a global phenomenon, a position he would never truly relinquish for the rest of his career? It all comes down to *Born To Run*, of course, but what makes this album so different from *Greetings From Asbury Park, N.J.* and *The Wild, The Innocent & The E Street Shuffle*?

To answer that question, it makes sense to look at the hallmarks of the first two albums and then to see how they have been transformed in *Born To Run*.

Most obviously, in the first two albums, there's the milieu that Springsteen has created. The location is blue-collar, urban East Coast, specifically New Jersey and New York. Menace and crime lurk on every street corner, and things can go from not that bad to really bad very quickly. It's night more often than it is day, a time when motorcycles and souped-up cars can take over the city's backstreets.

But in the third album, these backstreets feel more real. They're more carefully drawn, more poetic. The 'skeleton frames of burned-out Chevrolets' in 'Thunder Road' isn't just a rhyme for 'the boys you sent away'. It's a stark description of urban decay that is both evocative and accurately depicted. The songs continue to be populated by down-on-their-luck individuals, but the characters in *Born To Run* feel far more like real people. Instead of Crazy Janey and Sloppy Sue, we have Mary, Terry and Wendy. Sure, in some ways, they are stereotypical working-class Catholic girls, more the object of the speaker's desire than three-dimensional people. And yet generations of women have seen themselves in the females of these eight songs. On countless fan forums, and in books like *For You: Original Stories And Photographs By Bruce Springsteen's Legendary Fans*, women argue that there's something real, true and complex about these female characters, aspects of which will be explored in the individual song entries below. Overall, as Springsteen wrote in *Songs*, in *Born To Run*, characters of both genders tend to lose their more bizarre qualities. They have become 'less eccentric … They could have been anybody and everybody.'

Musically, pianos continue to play an important role in nearly every song, and not surprisingly, as Springsteen notes in *Songs*, the 'orchestral sound of *Born To Run* came from most of the songs being written on the piano.' There's a nuance, a depth of feeling that an electric guitar can't quite reach, but which newly-hired pianist Roy Bittan evokes effortlessly. His style and reach are different from that of the departed David Sancious: Bittan is a rock 'n' roll piano player, even if he is one whose talents far outstrip those of most of his contemporaries.

But *Born To Run* is far from being a 'piano album'. While electric guitars were important on the previous album on songs like 'Kitty's Back' and 'Rosalita', on the third album, they are an essential part of the 'Wall of Sound' that Springsteen, Appel and new producer Jon Landau tried to create partly in homage to Phil Spector's 1960s girl group records.

As to that 'Wall of Sound', it's hardly the 'little symphonies for kids', as Spector described his work with The Crystals and The Ronettes. Instead, in his autobiography, Springsteen talks about wanting to 'sound like Roy Orbison singing Bob Dylan, produced by Spector.' Technically, what the producers and engineer Louis Lahav did was compress and layer instruments on top of one another, the way that David Sancious had layered the playing of the three violinists on 'New York City Serenade' until they sounded like the strings in a small symphony orchestra. They did this, in part, by placing multiple instruments on individual tracks of the 16-track mixing deck. According to Springsteen, the title song had 72 separate tracks squeezed into the mixer's 16 tracks. And, of course, Springsteen's voice, as it was and would so often be on record, was enhanced by reverb.

In his book, *Springsteen*, Robert Hilburn writes: '*Born To Run* breathed with the same kind of discovery that made Elvis Presley's *Sun Sessions* and Bob Dylan's *Highway 61 Revisited* the two most important rock albums before it. Listening to all three works, you feel present at the forging of a major artistic vision. You sense the artist's excitement at finding something within himself that he hadn't known was there until it burst forth in the studio.'

When one thinks of the great rock acts of the 1960s and 1970s, it wasn't unusual for an artist to take a few albums to reach their potential. Sure, there were superb first albums that seemed to explode out of nowhere – *The Velvet Underground & Nico*, *The Doors*, King Crimson's *In The Court Of The Crimson King*, Jimi Hendrix's *Are Your Experienced?* in the 1960s, and Patti Smith's *Horses*, Elvis Costello's *My Aim Is True* and Television's *Marquee Moon* in the 1970s – but *Rubber Soul* was The Beatles sixth studio album, just as *Highway 61 Revisited* was Dylan's. *Blue* was Joni Mitchell's fourth album, and while *After The Gold Rush* was Neil Young's third solo album, he had released three others with Buffalo Springfield. Columbia was reportedly considering dropping Springsteen because of the poor sales of his first two records. Luckily, they realized his commercial potential before they made that grave mistake.

The album did not come together quickly like the two previous records, in part because of Springsteen's massive ambitions for *Born To Run*, and in part because his relationship with his manager/producer Mike Appel was unraveling. Stepping into the breach was Jon Landau, a music journalist, who famously wrote after watching Springsteen perform live in 1974, 'I saw rock 'n' roll's future and its name is Bruce Springsteen.' The two clicked. Springsteen writes in his autobiography that the only person he has shared more of his thoughts with is his wife, Patty Scialfa. In the film *Wings To Wheels: The Making Of Born To Run*, Landau comes across as more of a defender of the artiste, the man looking to make sure Springsteen's every last creative impulse is realized, while Appel, for all his gruffness, rightly just wants to get the record done.

Like so much else about *Born To Run*, the album's cover has become iconic. The black and white photograph by Eric Meola shows Springsteen in a black leather jacket and a torn white T-shirt, wearing a shark's tooth necklace, smiling and leaning against the back of an unknown person. For the first time on an album cover, we see Springsteen's famous guitar, already battered: a Telecaster body with a Fender Esquire neck. The big button pinned to Springsteen's guitar strap is tilted at an angle, but it shows the smiling face of Elvis Presley surrounded by the phrases, 'Elvis the King Fan Club of N.Y.C.' and 'King's Court Elvis Presley'.

The back cover reveals that the person on whom Springsteen is resting is none other than the Big Man, Clarence Clemons, who is blowing into his tenor saxophone. To the left of Clemons are the song titles and performer credits. When you open the album up, there's a black and white photo of a bearded Springsteen pushing back his black curly hair. The lyrics are printed in a small light gray font on a white background. You need to bend close to the jacket to take them all in.

Contemporary reviews of the album were glowing. Writing in the *Village Voice*, cranky Robert Christgau was won over, calling the album 'the fulfillment of everything 'Be My Baby' was about and lots more.' John Rockwell of *The New York Times* said it was 'one of the great records of recent years.' In *Rolling Stone*, Greil Marcus, previously a Springsteen skeptic, called *Born To Run* 'a magnificent album that pays off on every bet ever placed on him – a '57 Chevy running on melted down Crystals records that shuts down every claim that has been made.' Lester Bangs wrote in *Creem*: 'Street-punk image, bardic posture and all, Bruce Springsteen is an American archetype, and *Born To Run* will probably be the finest record released this year.' To top it all off, on 27 October 1975, Springsteen appeared simultaneously on the covers of *Time* and *Newsweek* magazines.

In *Born To Run*, the book, Springsteen says of *Born To Run*, the album: 'I'd loosely imagined [it] as a series of vignettes taking place during one long summer day and night.' He goes on to describe how each song adds to the story and concludes: 'At record's end, our lovers from 'Thunder Road' have had their early hard-won optimism severely tested by the streets of my noir city. They're left in fate's hands, in a land where ambivalence reigns and tomorrow is unknown.' Those are pretty grand sentiments, especially coming from the composer himself, but if ever an album lived up to its hype, this is the one.

'Thunder Road' (Springsteen)

While 'Thunder Road' was released as a single, it did not chart in the US or the UK. Yet it may be the Boss's best-known, or at least most beloved, song among all but his most casual fans. It's not hard to see why. Anyone who has attended a Springsteen concert has probably heard him play the song – by one count, he's performed it more than 1,400 times. Indeed, knowing all the words to 'Thunder Road' is a rock 'n' roll badge of honor, akin to being able to sing along faithfully to 'Stairway To Heaven' or 'Bohemian Rhapsody'.

'Thunder Road' (the title comes from a 1958 Robert Mitchum movie Springsteen only saw the poster for) is a love story about the narrator and Mary – and how much better that straightforward Catholic name is for this song than others Springsteen considered: Anne, Angelina, Christina and – egad! – Chrissie. However, their relationship, in the language of social media, is 'complicated'. The singer knows Mary well enough to invite her to leave her whole life behind and come with him, but he also knows she's 'lonely for words' he hasn't spoken. Moreover, she seems to have a number of other suitors. She can 'make crosses' from her lovers when she's lying in bed, and 'there were ghosts in the eyes of all the boys [she] sent away'. But those boys don't seem to be going quietly: 'They scream your name at night in the street./Your graduation gown lies in rags at their feet'. And yet, of course, it's that ambivalence that makes the song, like any good poem, so rewarding.

'Thunder Road' begins with the screen door slamming behind Mary as she walks out onto the front porch of her home and ends with the singer imploring her to climb inside his car so that she can join him in leaving their 'town full of losers' as he is 'pulling out of here to win'. In between those opening and closing moments, the story is much clearer than in any previous Springsteen song. On the first two albums, he seemed to embrace narrative distractions, following his rhyming dictionary wherever it led. Now, he is truly the boss of his own lyrics. Even ancillary details, like the fact that he's learned how to make his guitar 'talk', are used as evidence to persuade Mary that she ought to throw in her lot with the singer.

There's no chorus, but 'Thunder Road' does contain memorable lines in every verse. No one is likely to soon forget 'All the redemption I can offer is beneath this dirty hood'. Or: 'We're riding out tonight to case the promised land'. Or: 'From your front porch to my front seat,/The door's open but the ride ain't free'. Or, above all: 'You ain't a beauty, but, hey, you're all right', which Julia Roberts once said in an interview was the song lyric that best described her. Lines that would be the highlight of most songs – for instance, 'We got one last chance to make it real,/To trade in these wings on some wheels', where it's simply *implied* that the two main characters are fallen angels – are simply the fabric of this remarkable song. What's especially compelling is Springsteen's use of precise imagery, like the 'front porch' and his car's 'dirty hood', or the way casual locutions like 'hey, you're all right' take on the quality of enigmatic pronouncements – not to mention the Biblical allusion of the promised land. It's heady stuff for a high school graduate from Freehold, New Jersey.

And while it's easy to focus on the brilliance of the lyrics, the melody is equally superb. Were it being played only on guitar, much of 'Thunder Road' would be just a three-chord song; it's Roy Bittan's piano playing (the first time we've heard him on record) that makes the song so special. Live, Springsteen sometimes performs the song with only Bittan. (Check out the version on *Live/1975-1985* to see just how well this arrangement works.) The piano is indeed 'the magic in the night' that creates the mood in which the lyrics flourish.

That is not to downplay the contributions of the other musicians. Springsteen's opening harmonica is simple yet moving. Max Weinberg (also new to the band) is a steady hand at the drums. If we no longer hear 'Mad Dog' Lopez's occasional flourishes, they aren't really missed. Bittan's turn on the glockenspiel, an instrument Springsteen would continue to employ artfully throughout the 1970s and 1980s, adds another note of poignance. Then there's Springsteen's deep strata of electric guitar parts, which producer

John Landau claims took 13 hours of studio time to record. Finally, in the coda, which had been a mid-song instrumental break until Landau suggested moving it to the end, we have Clarence Clemons's joyously layered saxophones sounding the triumphant notes that assure us the two lovers are now on the road together. Mary has, indeed, 'climbed in'.

'Tenth Avenue Freeze Out' (Springsteen)
'Tenth Avenue Freeze-Out' was the second single released (in January 1976), after the title track. It peaked at a distinctly unimpressive number 83 on the *Billboard* Hot 100 and didn't chart at all in the UK. Other than its radio-friendly length of 3:11, it's an odd choice as the second-best song on *Born To Run*.

Which is not to say it isn't a great rock and soul number. The horn section was arranged by Steven Van Zandt, reunited with Springsteen after their time together in Steel Mill. Although Van Zandt had joined the touring E Street Band as second guitarist the month before the album's release, his only contributions to *Born To Run* are background vocals on 'Thunder Road', and this amazing horn chart, one which he more or less created on the fly after the horn players turned up only to learn; in Randy Brecker's words, 'They hadn't figured out what they wanted.'

Fortunately, Van Zandt had a stellar group of musicians to work with: Clarence Clemons on tenor saxophone, Randy Brecker on trumpet and bugle, Michael Brecker on tenor saxophone, Dave Sanborn on baritone sax and Wayne Andre on trombone. The song is impossible to imagine without the brass's constant musical commentary on Springsteen's lyrics. Sometimes, the horns seem to be enthusiastically endorsing Springsteen's concerns; other times, they almost seem to be teasing him, but overall, they are full of E Street funk and rhythm and blues.

Granted, not everyone is taken with 'Tenth Avenue Freeze Out', which is in sharp musical and lyrical contrast to the majesty of 'Thunder Road'. Writing in the *New Musical Express* in 1975, Andrew Tyler derided a 'melody and arrangement that is a patchwork of some of the more dubious R&R mannerisms of the early 1960s'. However, most listeners have heard, instead, what June Skinner Sawyers calls in *Tougher Than The Rest*, 'a buoyant, street-wise party song that celebrates life at its fullest … a festive, triumphant celebration of camaraderie in all its levels.'

Lyrically, that camaraderie centers on the relationship between Bad Scooter, a stand-in for Springsteen, and the Big Man, Clarence Clemons's nickname. In the first verse, Scooter feels like he 'can't find the room to move', that he's 'running on the bad side' with his 'back to the wall'. Things get even hairier in the second verse, when he is 'stranded in the jungle' before walking into a Tenth Avenue freeze-out, at which point he is, as Springsteen sings in the bridge, 'all alone' and 'can't go home'.

But then, as the ecstatic horns have been promising all along, good news arrives: 'The change was made uptown/And the Big Man joined the band'.

Suddenly, everything is all right, as 'from the coastline to the city/All the little pretties raise their hands', with the singer sitting back and laughing at his good fortune. It's a happy ending to what is certainly the most upbeat and optimistic song on an album where, otherwise, mistrust, uncertainty and bad luck tend to reign.

'Night' (Springsteen)

At just over three minutes, 'Night' is the shortest track on the album. The song begins and ends with Clemons blowing hard, if briefly, on his sax. In between, there's a rush of words lamenting the rigors of the working life, which Springsteen has acknowledged countless times he never actually experienced, along with the joys of getting in a hot rod (or on a motorcycle) and barreling down the highway to find 'a beautiful one' to lose your heart to. The lyrics harken back to a favorite Springsteen song, the Easybeats' 'Friday On My Mind', in which the singer laments, 'I know of nothing else that bugs me/More than working for the rich man', as he counts down the days to the weekend.

'Night' makes extensive use of suspended chords, which give the otherwise familiar chords a slightly 'off' feel, reflecting the song's focus on the difference between the hard work of daytime and the sensual pleasures of the night. And Springsteen uses another musical trick to emphasize that difference. The lines 'you work all day' and 'you work nine to five' at the end of the first two verses are sung over a B minor chord. However, in the lines that end the verses – 'To blow 'em away in the night' and 'Somehow you survive till the night' – he shifts to a B major, moving from a feeling of sorrow and angst to one of triumph and power.

The 'Wall of Sound' is in full force on 'Night'. In a *Rolling Stone* interview with David Fricke, engineer Jimmy Iovine noted, 'You can't really pick out what's playing' unless 'you listen closely'. In addition to the numerous guitar tracks, what stands out to the careful listener are Roy Bittan's piano, harpsicord and glockenspiel, which engage in hand-to-hand combat with Springsteen's riffing, and Gary Tallent's throbbing bassline.

Had it been released as the second single, 'Night' might have charted higher than 'Tenth Avenue Freeze-Out', although, inevitably, it would have been compared unfavorably to 'Born To Run', another, much richer song about escaping the 'rat traps' for a better life somewhere else.

'Backstreets' (Springsteen)

'Backstreets' begins with one of Roy Bittan's signature piano showcases. It's sad yet somehow struck through with notes of optimism. Tallent plays an understated bassline, and 50 seconds in, Bittan adds organ for another half-minute. It's a great setup for the lyrics that are about to follow.

As it is throughout *Born To Run*, the writing on 'Backstreets' is leaner and more condensed than on the previous albums. It's also more mysterious –

what, anyway, is a 'soft infested summer'? – and more inventive. Who, before Springsteen, could conjure up an image like 'dancers scraped the tears/Up off the streets'? Sure, the story is familiar, a young urban relationship gone sour, but the lines, like 'all the movies' the singer and Terry used to see, are cinematic in their sweep.

There's an ongoing debate about whether Terry is female or male, a lover or just a friend. The latter interpretation is supported by Springsteen himself in a 1984 interview with *Hot Press* magazine, where he said that numbers like 'Backstreets', along with 'No Surrender' and 'Bobby Jean' from *Born In The U.S.A.*, are 'just songs about friendship … They're just songs about people passing through, the rites of passage together'. Moreover, the Terry of 'The Promise' – a song recorded at this time but not released until 2010 – *appears* to be male, though that's not certain.

However, while Springsteen references gay life, especially in his early work, he never writes from an explicitly gay point of view. And 'Backstreets', unlike 'No Surrender' and 'Bobby Jean', indicates several times that there is an erotic element to the couple's relationship. In addition to 'sleeping in that old abandoned beach house' (okay, they could be *just* sleeping), they have 'a love so hard and filled with defeat', and they slow dance 'in the dark/On the beach at Stockton's Wing', where in 'the deep heart of the night', they 'let loose of everything'. Moreover, Terry is, in the final verse, 'Laying here in the dark … like an angel on [his] chest'. And if it's simply a close heterosexual male friendship, then why does the singer hate both Terry and the man she's gone away with in the third verse?

Ultimately, the nature of their relationship doesn't really matter, of course, though it would have been quite a lyrical breakthrough if 'Backstreets' had been the Boss's first gay love song. Whatever the interpretation, betrayal is at the heart of the relationship's dissolution. In the late 1970s, during live performances, Springsteen would add an interlude in the middle of the song, which fans called 'Sad Eyes'. Sometimes using the words and music to what would become *The River*'s 'Drive All Night', he would repeat 'Sad Eyes', as though he were addressing someone in the audience who, like Terry, had deceived him.

If there is a problem with this otherwise magnificent song, it's the many repetitions of 'Hiding on the backstreets' in the final section. Springsteen sings the same line, not counting the one slight variation with the word 'tonight', 25 times. Initially, we can feel his pain. The singer is so heartbroken over his break-up with Terry and the breakdown in his life that he must keep howling the line to expel the anguish in which he is engulfed. But it goes on and on and on and on and on until the repetition begins to sound unintentionally comic toward the end. 'All right, already', one wants to say toward the end, 'I get it: you're hiding on the backstreets.'

Ultimately, language gives way to guttural wails and moans – an expression of pure emotion to which the song has been aspiring all along. Then, finally, with bass, drums and piano ushering it home, 'Backstreets' slows and stops, and side one of this astonishing album comes to its conclusion.

'Born To Run' (Springsteen)

While other tracks on later albums went higher on the charts, 'Born To Run' is Springsteen's signature song. It is his 'My Generation', his 'Like A Rolling Stone', his 'Stairway To Heaven', his 'Hotel California', his 'Sweet Child O' Mine', his 'Smells Like Teen Spirit'. It is the title of his most important album and of his autobiography, and the story it tells, of a young man and woman breaking free of the world they were born in to go off in a possibly futile search for liberty and happiness, is his quintessential rock 'n' roll myth.

In his autobiography, Springsteen says that he wrote the song 'sitting on the edge of my bed in a cottage I'd newly rented … in Long Branch, New Jersey. I was in the midst of giving myself a crash tutorial in 1950s and 1960s rock 'n' roll. I had a small table holding a record player at the side of my cot, so I was just one drowsy roll away from dropping the needle onto my favorite album of the moment.'

The lyrics developed through various live performances, and part of the song was recorded in the old, semi-decrepit studio in Blauvelt before Landau convinced Springsteen and Columbia to move the recording for the rest of *Born To Run* to the Record Plant on West 44th Street in Manhattan. 'Born To Run' was the first song recorded for the album. Springsteen always knew the crucial role the song would play, 'sequenced dead in the middle of the record, anchoring all that comes before and after.'

Wendy, the heroine of 'Born To Run', is different from Mary in 'Thunder Road' and Terry in 'Backstreets' in that she is a purer embodiment of the singer's desire. Mary was involved with other young men, and Terry left the singer altogether, but Wendy seems to offer the possibility of true love, and, more importantly, companionship. Not only does the singer want to be Wendy's friend, but he wants to 'guard [her] dreams and visions'. Together, the two of them can break the 'trap' that has ensnared them. If she agrees to their compact, they will walk together 'out on the wire' and learn to 'live with the sadness'. Granted, for the moment, they are still born to run, but there's a better place out there beyond the Jersey Shore, a place where they can 'walk in the sun'. Despite all the caveats and qualifications and provisos, 'Born To Run' is a song about escape and about hope.

With dozens and dozens of tracks layered atop one another, 'Born To Run' takes full advantage of the 'Wall of Sound'. Nevertheless, beyond Springsteen's army of guitars, we can pick out individual instruments, most notably the glockenspiel, an instrument heard in Stravinsky's *Firebird* and Mahler's Sixth and Eighth Symphonies, which, in Roy Bittan's hands, plays a crucial role in this grittiest of rock songs.

And then, of course, there is Clarence Clemons's iconic saxophone solo. After the second verse and before the bridge, he gives us 20 seconds of unadulterated jubilance. He also leads the band in the post-bridge instrumental that takes us to a false ending after which Springsteen shouts out, in a commanding voice that surely inspired Joey Ramone, 'One, two, three, four!'

At four and a half minutes, 'Born To Run' is a bit longer than the average top 40 song of the time, but every moment is full of excitement and energy. Springsteen's five-note riff is the perfect hook, and the band, as numerous commentators have noted, never sounded better. That's interesting because two key musicians play only on this one song. 'Born To Run' was drummer Ernest 'Boom' Carter's only song with Springsteen. A friend of Sancious's from Asbury Park, Carter stepped in during the interim after Lopez left the band and before Weinstein was hired. This was also David Sancious's final recording with the band. 'He'd soon be offered his own solo deal on Columbia', Springsteen writes in his autobiography. 'Right before the gravy train!' Although Sancious did return, decades later, for appearances on *Human Touch* (1992) and *Western Stars* (2019), his jazzier style, for better or worse, would be largely missing from the E Street Band.

'She's The One' (Springsteen)

'She's the One' begins with some low strumming – if you're not listening carefully, it almost sounds like someone humming for the first five seconds – then Bittan comes in strong on the electric harpsichord, as Springsteen sings the virtues of a woman with 'killer graces' and 'secret places/That no boy can fill'. She has 'her hands on her hips/Oh, and that smile on her lips/Because she knows that it kills [him]'.

Basically, the woman is a dream, or an angel, something not of this world, and as the first verse continues, it's all over-the-top, reverb-drenched praise from Springsteen, accompanied only by the harpsichord and periodic strums of the guitar.

We hear twice that 'She's the one', then Springsteen hollers, 'Ha!', and drums, bass and a more pronounced guitar join in on the Bo Diddley beat. After the second verse, there's a short bridge with some funky guitar playing, and then it's Big Man time. Springsteen claims in his memoir that he wrote the song 'just so I could hear C blow that sax solo over the top of it.' And though it's buried a bit in the mix, Clemons's saxophone once again shakes off the incipient sadness of the lyrics and makes the song sound like a celebration, even though it seems pretty likely that 'she' is never going to be the subject of a long-term romance. It sounds so free and spontaneous, yet every note of the solo had been dictated by Springsteen.

'She's The One' is the exact same length as 'Born To Run, but whereas every second of the title track seems essential, after Clemons's solo ends at 3:34, the drum-heavy vamping in the final minute feels less essential – it's certainly fun, and in the spirit of Springsteen's live shows – but not as *vital* as the first three-quarters of the song.

Like 'Night', 'She's The One' makes extensive use of suspended chords, and like that song, it feels both satisfying and yet a little 'off', throbbing with a frisson that keeps it from feeling like the centerpiece of the album.

'Meeting Across The River' (Springsteen)

Slow or fast, every track up to this point has been a rock song. Suddenly, we're hit with a forlorn blast of trumpet, played by Randy Brecker, and some blue notes on the piano from Bittan, and we're in an entirely different musical, if not lyrical, world.

'Meeting Across The River' is sung by an unnamed man to his friend Eddie. The singer is asking Eddie for 'a few bucks', and a ride through the tunnel from New Jersey into Manhattan, where he has 'a meeting with a man on the other side'. The two men have evidently made some bad choices in the past and upset some powerful people. Tonight is their last chance to redeem themselves, and the singer reminds Eddie that 'if we blow this one/They ain't gonna be looking for just me this time'.

These are two low-class losers. Not only do they not have enough money to make it into Manhattan, but they have no weapon – the singer advises Eddie to stuff something into his pocket so 'It'll look like you're carrying a friend'. They have to remember to change their shirts (and not smile) so they look like they 'got style', but they are, in fact, dead broke. The singer even had to hock his girlfriend's radio for, presumably, 'a few bucks' that he's already spent.

The worlds of New Jersey and New York have sometimes flowed into one another on other songs, but in 'Meeting Across The River', it's clear that the New Yorkers have the power, and the Jerseyites are subservient. And yet in a 2005 *Rolling Stone* interview with Brian Hiatt, Springsteen clearly indicates that he has sympathy for his two shifty characters, who live so close to the Big City, but are far from comfortable when they are actually on its streets: 'It's funny because, back then, when you lived in New Jersey, you could've been a million miles from New York City and yet it was always there ... So that song grew out of, 'Hey, that guy's sort of a small-time player, but he's still got his sights set on what's across that river.' I suppose that was where the emotions of it came from.'

Throughout the song, Brecker's trumpet evokes the film noir world Springsteen has been trying to depict in his words, while Bittan's piano keeps the story moving. Jazz double bassist Richard Davis, who had played on both Eric Dolphy's *Out To Lunch!* and Van Morrison's *Astral Weeks*, as well as 'The Angel' on *Asbury Park*, brings a sophisticated, understated sound in his role.

The closest musical cousin to 'Meeting Across The River' on *Born To Run* is probably 'Tenth Avenue Freeze-Out'. However, while the horns on the side one song jumped and shimmied, the lone horn part on 'Meeting Across The River' is as ghostly and evocative as a streetlight on an empty alleyway.

Including 'Meeting Across The River' on *Born To Run* was daring on Springsteen's part. The song completely changes the mood of the album from rock 'n' roll to bluesy jazz. Yet Springsteen knew what he was doing. Listeners needed to slow down and catch their breath before encountering the album's final masterwork.

'Jungleland' (Springsteen)

What is it about 'Jungleland' that makes it so much more monumental than 'New York City Serenade', the equally ambitious closing track on *The Wild, The Innocent & The E Street Shuffle*? Both songs feature impressive instrumental sections and depict mostly nocturnal urban environments. However, 'Jungleland' not only tells a more coherent story, but it does so, in the opinion of many critics, including this one, in language that is among the most memorable ever written for a rock 'n' roll song.

What insight and word painting there are in lines like 'The kids round here live just like shadows,/Always quiet, holding hands' and 'Kids flash guitars just like switch-blades,/Hustling for the record machine'. Like Springsteen himself, in Jungleland, 'The hungry and the hunted/Explode into rock 'n' roll bands'. It's a world both separate unto itself, and yet, as the song's enduring popularity attests, one in which listeners from vastly different places can imagine themselves inhabiting.

The band had been playing 'Jungleland' live since March 1974, during which time it underwent changes both musically and lyrically. In the latter case, Springsteen's constant revisions were nearly always improvements. To take just one example, cited by Peter Ames Carlin in his biography *Bruce*, in the penultimate stanza, the line was originally 'In the tunnel of machines you'll hear the screams drowned out by the trains'. By the autumn of 1974, it had become 'In the tunnel of machines the magic Rat chases his dreams'. That's better, at least we have the Magic Rat, a character introduced in the first verse, returning to the song, but Springsteen nails it in the final version: 'In the tunnels uptown, the Rat's own dream guns him down'. The Rat dying is far more poignant than having him simply chase his dreams. And the response from the onlookers to the Rat's death – no one watching 'when the ambulance pulls away/Or as the girl shuts out the bedroom light' – is, like the slowly building strings at that point in the song, eerie and nearly bursting with unexpressed grief. The moment is nearly operatic in its sweep and effectiveness.

What follows that near-silence is one of the Boss's greatest verses, one worth quoting in full, lyrics which Springsteen sings with indisputable authority:

Outside the street's on fire in a real death waltz
Between what's flesh and what's fantasy
And the poets down here
Don't write nothing at all
They just stand back and let it all be
And in the quick of the knife they reach for their moment

And try to make an honest stand
But they wind up wounded, not even dead
Tonight in Jungleland

The difference between 'what's flesh and what's fantasy' is a crucial one, not only for the song, but for Springsteen himself. His whole musical career up to this point has been a blending of things he has only seen or imagined with his actual lived life.

Then there's the superb passage 'the poets down here/Don't write nothing at all/They just stand back and let it all be'. These lines both give voice to Springsteen's aesthetic – he is an observer above all – while simultaneously separating him from the denizens of his youth. After all, throughout 'Jungleland', *Born To Run* and his entire corpus, this self-described 'obsessive/compulsive' is assiduously capturing, *on paper*, the details of the New Jersey/New York life he can't quite leave behind.

Finally, there's the hurried line, 'in the quick of the knife they reach for their moment', where 'knife', the gatefold of the album tells us, is the actual word, not the expected 'night'. What a subtle and devastating sleight of hand, followed by the unanticipated sorrow we feel for the poets when they end up wounded but still living, 'not even dead', not going out in the blaze of glory they would have wanted.

The instrumental elements are striking in themselves. We begin with Suki Lahav, who, by the end of the album, has moved back to Israel with her engineer husband Louis, who has given the controls over to Jimmy Iovine. She plays a beautiful violin opening that accompanies Roy Bittan's piano, and when we reach the end of the second verse, Bittan's organ comes surging through, and soon the guitars, bass and drums have turned a piano ballad into a full-on rock song, complete with what would become one of Springsteen's most recognizable guitar solos.

There's a bridge, things slow down, and then ... *the saxophone solo*. According to Carlin in his book *Tonight In Jungleland: The Making Of Born To Run*, when engineer Jimmy Iovine talks about the solo, it 'makes his eyes widen and his mouth drop open. 'Oh, yeah, are you kidding me? Not only did he put Clarence through the wringer, but I also recorded every note of it." Springsteen, Carlin writes, 'talked Clemons through each note and passage, had him play them all individually, then together.' But even after 'Clemons really had mastered the part, was playing his heart out', Springsteen kept asking for another take, and another, and another, for many hours on end.

But it was worth it. When the solo is over, we move into the final two verses described above. Then the last 55 seconds are given over to a musical coda highlighted by piano, strings and bass, punctuated by Springsteen's 'wordless wails', which Melissa Etheridge described as 'the definition of rock 'n' roll to me.' The strings fade out and *Born To Run* has made an inarguable case for its greatness.

Darkness On The Edge Of Town (1978)

Personnel:

Bruce Springsteen: lead vocals, lead guitar; harmonica ('The Promised Land')

Roy Bittan: piano, backing vocals ('Adam Raised A Cain')

Clarence Clemons: saxophone ('Badlands', 'The Promised Land' and 'Prove It All Night'), percussion ('Badlands', 'Adam Raised A Cain', 'Racing In The Street', 'Factory', and 'Darkness On The Edge Of Town'), backing vocals ('Badlands' and 'Adam Raised A Cain')

Danny Federici: Hammond organ, glockenspiel ('Something In The Night' and 'Candy's Room'), backing vocals ('Adam Raised A Cain')

Garry Tallent: bass guitar, backing vocals ('Adam Raised A Cain')

Steven Van Zandt: rhythm guitar, backing vocals (except 'The Promised Land' and 'Darkness On The Edge Of Town')

Max Weinberg: drums, backing vocals ('Adam Raised A Cain')

Recorded at The Record Plant, New York City, between June 1977 and March 1978

Producers: Bruce Springsteen and Jon Landau

Release date: 2 June 1978

Running time: 42:29

Label: Columbia

Album charts: US: 5, UK: 14

Singles charts: 'Prove It All Night' (US: 33); 'Badlands' (US: 42)

When writing about *Darkness On The Edge Of Town*, it's tempting to get caught up in the story of its creation and lose sight of the album itself. Nevertheless, it's worth providing some background, as the process clearly had an effect on the writing and recording of the material that ended up on the record.

Following the success of *Born To Run*, it was time for Springsteen to renew his contract with Mike Appel and Laurel Canyon Productions. When Springsteen had signed with Appel, he was more concerned with making it in the business than with the financial issues success might bring. However, when Appel presented him with a new contract, Springsteen took it to a lawyer who famously said the only contract he'd seen that was worse was that of Frankie Lymon, the doo wop singer who had been cheated of his fortune.

Springsteen refused to sign the contract and fired Appel, but their previous contract stipulated that only Appel could name the producer of Springsteen's next album. As a result, the singer refused to go back into the studio until he was able to take control of his songs and his career.

Ultimately, Springsteen bought Appel out, regaining ownership of the songs on his first three albums. During the protracted legal battle, Springsteen and the E Street Band rehearsed at Springsteen's home, while Springsteen wrote song after song, and when the group returned to the Record Plant, with John

Landau by Springsteen's side as producer, they began to record his new material. By one count in the film *The Promise: The Making Of Darkness On The Edge Of Town*, the E Street Band taped 70 songs for the album (though Springsteen himself says it was 60), a trend of songwriting overkill that would continue for the rest of Springsteen's career, although he would never again be quite as prolific as he was in the mid- and late 1970s.

A few of these *Darkness*-era unreleased songs went to other artists. 'Fire', written for Elvis Presley, who died in August 1977, was a number two hit for The Pointer Sisters in 1979, and 'Because The Night' was Patti Smith's only top 40 Hit. Some of the songs ended up on other albums, like *The River – The Promise* film contains a hilarious sequence in which Springsteen plays piano and sings 'Sherry Darling' while Steven Van Zandt pounds on the piano top with drumsticks – while other numbers didn't drop until many years later. The *Tracks* boxset from 1998 contains a sampling of these, and 2010's *The Promise* contains another 20.

With so much quality material on hand, Springsteen was constantly changing his mind about the album's contents. During the recording sessions, the band placed bets on which songs Springsteen was going to take out of the album that day, and which ones he was going to reintroduce.

In the event, both 'Fire' and 'The Promise', which had generally been shortlisted, were left off. Springsteen was keen to ensure that the album, which Landau lauded as the ultimate rock 'n' roll art form, held together as a coherent collection of songs, and *Darkness On The Edge Of Town* certainly does that. In his autobiography, Springsteen says he cut 'the massive block of songs to the ten toughest. I edited out anything that broke the album's mood or tension.' Calling it his 'samurai record, all stripped down for fighting', he eschewed 'anything that smacked of frivolity or nostalgia.'

The *Darkness* songs present us with many of the same types of people we'd met on *Born To Run*, but Springsteen was no longer 24 years old. He was 27 now, and concerned with the hard choices made by working-class adults. You might be 'born to run', but unless you die, sooner or later, you realize that you have nowhere to run to. You have to make your stand, even if it means admitting your failure. There's an edginess to these songs, and Springsteen writes in his autobiography that in 1978, 'I felt a distant kinship to [punk groups like the Sex Pistols and The Clash], to the class consciousness, the anger. They hardened my resolve.' The working-class connection was true enough, and he did sport something of a New Wave look during the album's tour, but Springsteen was too much of a perfectionist ever to be a punk.

Springsteen also began listening to Hank Williams, and country music's ability to speak to 'adult topics' clearly appealed to the Boss, although the *spirit* of the music is what's present here rather than its sound. There are some occasional country inflections in *The River*, and even more in *Nebraska*, but the *truly* country songs in Springsteen's catalogue are a long way off, in 2019's *Western Stars*.

Perhaps the debt to Hank Williams was as much structural as thematic. As Rob Kirkpatrick writes in *Magic In The Night*, 'Whereas the choruses on past albums sometimes serve as speed bumps to the runaway lyrics, the choruses on *Darkness* stay as the rallying cries of the songs. Indeed, Springsteen admitted that these songs tended to emerge from the chorus outward.' Mike Appel, possibly bitter over his dismissal, felt that Springsteen's gravitation toward more conventional songwriting sapped him of his unique creativity, and it's true his work around this time fits into a more standard vision of rock 'n' roll. However, there's no doubt that, in the coming years, as the lyrical odysseys gave way to verse-chorus-bridge songs, his popularity increased.

The front cover of the album presented us with the new, clean-shaven Springsteen. Shot by Frank Stefanko in his New Jersey home, it is a color photograph of Springsteen with curly uncombed hair, in a white T-shirt and a black leather jacket, leaning against Venetian blinds in a room with cabbage rose wallpaper. It could be one of the cheap motels or boarding houses in which his characters find themselves – it could even be Candy's room.

The reverse side shows him in the same room, at a slightly different angle, in just the T-shirt. This is before he began hitting the weights in the early 1980s, and he looks thin and vulnerable without his jacket. Inside the album was a lyric sheet, the ten songs typed up in typewriter font. 'All songs © 1978 Bruce Springsteen (ASCAP). All rights reserved'. There was no mistaking the boss of Springsteen's material.

Nearly three years after the release of *Born To Run*, *Darkness On The Edge Of Town* came out to the critical acclaim to which Springsteen was now accustomed, although reviews for his fourth album weren't *quite* as glowing as those for his third. Still, in the *Rolling Stone* review, Dave Marsh contended that 'Occasionally, a record appears that changes fundamentally the way we hear rock 'n' roll, the way it's recorded, the way it's played.' *Darkness*, featuring 'the E Street Band … clearly one of the finest rock 'n' roll groups ever assembled', was one such record. Writing in the *Village Voice*, Robert Christgau said the best songs on the album 'are models of how an unsophisticated genre can illuminate a mature, full-bodied philosophical insight. Lyrically and vocally, they move from casual to incantatory modes with breathtaking subtlety, jolting ordinary details into meaning.' The praise continued. *Creem*: 'artful, passionate, rigorous'. *Crawdaddy!*: 'unsettling' and 'staggering'. *The Chicago Tribune*: 'Springsteen brandishes his guitar and voice like blowtorches.'

The album reached number five in the US and number 14 in the UK. The three singles, however, did not fare as well. 'Prove It All Night' reached number 33, and 'Badlands' made it to number 42, but 'The Promised Land' did not crack the *Billboard* 100. None of the songs charted in the UK, although the *New Musical Express* named the album the best of 1978.

In *Born To Run,* Springsteen sums up the continuing importance of the album: 'The songs from *Darkness On The Edge Of Town* remain at the core of our live performances today and are perhaps the purest distillation of what I wanted my rock 'n' roll music to be about.'

'Badlands' (Springsteen)

'Three chords and the truth', composer Harlan Howard said in the 1950s when defining a great country song, and that phrase, of course, applies equally to rock 'n' roll. It's certainly apt for 'Badlands', which employs the great rock 'n' roll chords E, A and B, used in many classic songs of the 1950s, to tell a story of defiance in the face of despair.

The song's title is a nod to Terrance Malik's movie of the same name, although the story the film relates, of two young people committing murder across the American badlands, isn't told by Springsteen until the title song on *Nebraska*. Instead, 'Badlands' is about a man facing up to hard times but refusing to give in to them. The singer also frequently refers to a 'you'. Sometimes, this is clearly his beloved ('I believe in the love that you gave me'), but at other times, he seems to be singing to a much wider audience ('Workin' in the field/You get your back burned/Workin' 'neath the wheels/ You get your facts learned'). The Boss knows how carefully his devoted fans are listening to his every word, and as Rob Kirkpatrick points out in *Magic In The Night*, 'Springsteen begins to sing to a proverbial 'you' standing in for his audience.' The effect is to bring the singer and his listeners ever closer to one another.

The fifth verse alludes to an Elvis Presley song from 1962, 'King Of The Whole Wide World'. However, that song, written by Bob Roberts and Ruth Batchelor, is more about learning to live with what you don't have: 'A poor man wants to be a rich man/A rich man wants to be a king/But the man who can sing when he hasn't got a thing/He's the king of the whole wide world'. Springsteen, by contrast, doesn't want to sing; he wants to 'go out tonight' and 'find out what I got'.

Springsteen's interest in punk rock comes through in both his defiant attitude and in the music, which, despite the stellar piano playing of Roy Bittan and organist Gary Federci – back in the band after being entirely dropped from *Born To Run* – is driven by the hard-charging guitars of Springsteen and his old friend Steven Van Zandt, who had finally, officially, joined the E Street Band. It's a big, radio-friendly sound, but it's not a 'Wall of Sound'.

After the second chorus, there's a ripping guitar solo from the Boss for eight bars, then the Big Man takes 16 bars, changing the tone of the instrumental passage from anger to triumph. Interestingly, the saxophone solo wasn't added until the album was all but finished, and Springsteen decided there wasn't enough of Clemons on it. The music quietens after the solos, with Bittan's piano beneath a hummed 'mm mm mm' from Springsteen. However, that mellow interlude is only long enough for us and Springsteen to catch our breath before he hurls himself back into the melee and announces,

'I wanna find one face/That ain't looking through me/I wanna find one place/I wanna spit in the face of these/Badlands'.

At a South by Southwest event in 2012, Springsteen acknowledged that he'd taken the riff for 'Badlands' from The Animals' 'Don't Let Me Be Misunderstood': 'Listen up, youngsters! This is how successful theft is accomplished!' But the theft is successful only because the earlier song has been so thoroughly translated into Springsteen's own idiom.

'Adam Raised A Cain' (Springsteen)

If 'Badlands' gave a nod to the snarl of punk rock, 'Adam Raised A Cain' fully genuflects to it. The song begins with nine seconds of Springsteen playing the same note on his guitar, as if he's too angry to play anything else. He does, however, launch into a solo that makes clear that his electric guitar is the instrumental Boss of 'Adam Raised A Cain', with Max Weinberger's booming drums and Gary Tallent's thumping bass coming in a close second.

Springsteen doesn't sing the lyrics so much as he screams them, but pretty quickly we realize that the song's title isn't just a bad pun: it's about father-son relationships. Other than the author himself, the star of Springsteen's sprawling autobiography is his father, Douglas. A bitter man who, at least when Bruce was growing up in Freehold, seemed to resent his son far more than he ever loved him, Doug's cold war with his son may have been emotionally crippling to the younger Springsteen, but it proved to be great material for his songs.

Springsteen frequently mentions the influence of films on his songwriting, and we can see that inspiration in the way he shifts the scene from verse to verse. In the opening four lines, the singer's father is crying at his baptism. In the very next verse, the singer seems to be a teenager: his father stands in the doorway while the singer stands in the rain, 'the same hot blood burning in [their] veins'. Springsteen bellows the title four times, which is the chorus, then in the next two verses, the narrator seems to be an adult who has unexpectedly returned home – 'All of the old faces/Ask you why you're back' – but it's an unhappy homecoming, as the past intrudes on the singer, 'relentless as the rain'.

The guitar solo begins with the same machine-gunned note before it evolves into one of Springsteen's most memorable pieces of extended studio guitar playing. Then, he shouts, and everyone in the band shouts with him, before the lapsed Catholic boy gives us his most Scriptural verse to date: 'In the Bible Cain slew Abel/And east of Eden he was cast/You're born into this life paying/For the sins of somebody else's past'. In Exodus 20:5, God says, 'I am a jealous God, visiting the inequity of the fathers upon the children of the third and fourth generation of them that hate me'. And yet there is also Ezekiel 18:20: 'The son shall not bear the iniquity of the father, neither shall the father bear the iniquity of the son'. Still, Exodus fits better with Springsteen's own life experience, and in the final verse, there's a note of sympathy for the father with whom he cannot connect: 'Daddy worked his whole life for nothing but the pain/Now he walks these empty rooms looking for something to blame'.

When Springsteen was explaining to Chuck Plotkin, who stepped in to do some emergency mixing, how he wanted 'Adam Raised A Cain' to sound in relation to the songs around it, he used a cinematic metaphor. Imagine, he told Plotkin, a film with two lovers at a picnic. Suddenly, there's a jump cut to a corpse. This song is that corpse.

'Something In The Night' (Springsteen)

The tempo slows down considerably with 'Something In The Night'. At first, it's only Bittan's piano, then Tallent's bass and Federici's glockenspiel. The introduction is just two chords, but there's something unsettling amidst Bittan's beautiful playing, which increases dramatically when Springsteen begins his wordless moaning and wailing through the first minute of the song. Finally, that vocalese morphs into 'Whoa-oh-oh!' and soon we're in familiar space: at the wheel of a car on a New Jersey night. The singer is headed to a bar when suddenly he gets an itch to press the pedal to the metal, 'looking for a moment when the world seems right'.

But nothing much is right in the world of this song, as we learn in the second verse: 'Well, you're born with nothing/And better off that way/Soon as you got something they send/Someone to try and take it away'. In fact, it's possible to 'ride this road till dawn/Without another human being in sight'. No human beings, that is, except for 'wasted' kids, who apparently don't count.

The bridge, with Steven Van Zandt joining in on harmony vocals, continues to emphasize the desolate place in which the singer has found himself: 'Nothing is forgotten or forgiven/When it's your last time around'. And like so many other Springsteen characters, this one is living with a heavy load of guilt for some unnamed offense: 'I got stuff running 'round my head/That I just can't live down'.

The third and final verse, when the things the speaker loves are 'crushed and dying in the dirt', begins on a note so forlorn that the only instrumentation is Weinberg's stark and simple drumming. And then, with the band returning, we are back to the desolate 'Whoa-oh-oh!'s all the way to the end of the song.

What is the 'something in the night' that so haunts the singer? It's desirable, yes, but it's also elusive and ephemeral. And wherever it is, that 'something' is buried deep in the night, which Springsteen equates with death, surely, and depression, no doubt. But 'night' also seems to be an entity or situation more all-encompassing – an existential void, an abyss that sucks every ray of light into it. And yet Springsteen manages to concoct a pretty great rock song around emotional and physical disaster. The unknown 'they' may have burned his car and left him and his unnamed companion 'running burn and blind', but that doesn't keep the singer from continuing to chase 'something in the night'.

'Candy's Room' (Springsteen)

At 2:48, 'Candy's Room' is the length of a classic early 1960s 45 rpm record, but the structure of Springsteen's song is different from the verse-chorus-bridge we expect from such a song. Instead, 'Candy's Room' begins with Weinberg playing fast but soft on a closed hi-hat before Springsteen begins singing quietly, Bittan accompanying him with a delicate piano line. In the second verse, the band join in – guitars, bass, glockenspiel – with the drums continuing at their frenetic pace. Springsteen plays a gnarly lead guitar solo that will then echo the melody for the rest of the remaining two abbreviated verses. The song ends with a whispered 'Tonight' over the hushed piano and drums, but the guitar is still in the mix, reminding us, perhaps, of the singer's passionate, tortured feelings for Candy. It's a rollercoaster of a ride and far superior to the plodding version entitled 'Candy's Boy' that can be heard on 2010's *The Promise*.

When asked by *Rolling Stone* whether Candy was a prostitute, Springsteen replied: 'Does it matter?' Evidently not, though the character is so intriguing that we can't help but want to know more about her. To reach Candy's room, suitors must walk down a dark hall, where they will find 'pictures of her heroes on the wall' (in an earlier version, they were 'saviors'), along with the 'toys' and 'fancy clothes and diamond rings' previous men have brought her. She's obviously very attractive – just one kiss, and the singer feels not only the blood rushing in his veins, but fire rushing 'towards the sky' – and yet 'There's a sadness hidden in that pretty face/A sadness all her own, from which no man can keep Candy safe'.

Attaching real names to the fictional characters in Springsteen's songs is always something of a mug's game, but artist Karon Bihari told the not always reliable *National Enquirer*, 'When *Darkness* came out, there was a song about us called 'Candy's Room', and it just took my breath away … The lyrics described my little apartment, what we talked about, when we kissed.' She concludes: 'It was the most romantic thing anyone had ever done for me.'

That's an interesting statement because while the song is certainly a tribute to Candy, Springsteen makes no effort to idolize her. She's a woman who inspires great ardor in the singer and many other men, but she's also a flawed human being: in short, something like a real person.

'Racing In The Street' (Springsteen)

In the film *The Promise: The Making Of Darkness On The Edge Of Town*, Springsteen talks about how carefully he and producer Jon Landau thought about the 'corners' of a vinyl LP. The first and last songs on each side were the corners: the other songs worked within the confines of those important tracks. Partly what makes *Darkness* such a superb album is the indisputable greatness of its four corner songs: 'Badlands' and 'Racing In The Street' on side one, and 'The Promised Land' and 'Darkness On The Edge Of Town' on side two.

'Racing In The Street' is one of Springsteen's great lyrics, a happy medium between the loquaciousness of the first three albums and the sparer writing of albums to come. It also bridges the imaginal and the personal. In *Songs*, Springsteen writes: 'In 'Racing In The Street', I wanted my street racers to carry the years between the car songs of the 1960s and 1978 America. To make 'Racing' and those other big titles personal, I had to infuse the music with my own hopes and fears. If you don't do that, your characters ring hollow, and you're left with rhetoric, words without meaning.'

Springsteen, of course, never went around the country racing in the street with his 'partner Sonny', but we learn in *The Promise* movie that he did, indeed, have some experience riding shotgun during some street racing on the backroads of New Jersey. And we know from his autobiography that he owned a 1957 Chevy Bel Air, which had, as the song indicates, a Hurst shifter – 'a Hurst on the floor' – not to mention orange flames painted across the hood.

But mostly what Springsteen is channeling is the same loneliness that the driver of the fast car in 'Something In The Night' is trying to outrace. You can hear it in Bittan's pensive piano accompaniment, and in Federci's doleful organ, which kicks in toward the end of the second verse. When the narrator sings about the many triumphs he and Sonny have had, it is with resignation rather than the braggadocio of The Beach Boys in songs like 'Little Deuce Coupe': 'She's got a competition clutch with the four on the floor/And she purrs like a kitten till the lake pipes roar'.

In fact, the song might have become just another one of Springsteen's takes on fast cars if it weren't for the third verse, after Danny Federici's organ solo, which, for 20 seconds, has offered a glimpse of hope in the darkness. Instead, we learn that the singer has been living with a woman for the past three years after he beat her previous boyfriend, 'this dude from LA', in a race. But good times seem to be long gone now, as, with echoes of 'Candy's Room', there are 'wrinkles around my baby's eyes/And she cries herself to sleep at night'. As in 'Thunder Road' ('Tonight we'll be free, all the promises'll be broken') and 'Born To Run' ('We'll go to that place where we really want to go'), the answer the narrator has for his seemingly intractable romantic problems is to get his beloved into his car and drive away: 'Tonight my baby and me, we're gonna ride to the sea/And wash these sins off our hands'. Will this solve their problems? Probably not, but these songs are primarily about traveling, not reaching a destination.

The title and chorus allude to Martha and the Vandellas' 1964 hit, 'Dancing In The Street', written by Marvin Gaye, William Stevenson and Ivy Jo Hunter. That song, with its upbeat party vibe, is a call for people 'everywhere around the world' to go dancing in the street. In contrast, Springsteen's song, with its melancholy tempo and depressing lyrics, makes racing in the street sound like the opposite of fun – more a duty than a release.

As did nearly all the songs on *Darkness*, 'Racing In The Street' went through many permutations, both live and in the recording studio – according to Clinton Heylin in *Springsteen Song By Song*, there were 17 takes – before Springsteen decided on the final track.

You can hear one of those versions, 'Racing In The Street ('78)', on 2010's *The Promise*. The piano isn't nearly as fluid, and the narrator is driving a ''32 Ford' rather than a ''69 Chevy'. Springsteen's harmonica plays a larger role, and David Lindley plays a lovely violin solo. It's a good song, a lot livelier, but one thing we learn from nearly all the outtakes and alternate versions that came out decades after the original albums were released is what a sharp ear Springsteen has for the best song and the best rendition of that song. If, throughout his career, his albums have been far more successful than his singles, it's because he cherishes what, to many, is an antiquated format, but which, when it is working perfectly, as on *Darkness*, is hard to beat as a musical statement.

'The Promised Land' (Springsteen)

'Deep despair and resilience', Springsteen says of 'The Promised Land' at the end of *The Promise: The Making Of Darkness On The Edge Of Town*. The song is about 'Determination. Assessment of limitations. Desire to transcend limitations in the way that you can.'

Springsteen borrowed his song's title from a 1964 Chuck Berry tune, which recounts the singer's comically eventful trip across America from Norfolk, Virginia, to California ('the promised land'). Ironically, the song was written while Berry was in prison for violating the Mann Act – a statute punishing those taking minors across state lines for sexual purposes.

The phrase itself has been a key one for the Boss across his career. To take just one example, there is 'Thunder Road', where Mary and the singer are 'riding out tonight to case the promised land'. The allusion, of course, is to the Biblical promised land of Canaan, where milk and honey flowed for the fleeing Jewish people, and which was the subject, as June Skinner Sawyers points out in *Tougher Than The Rest*, of many 'spirituals adopted first by African slaves, then by African-Americans', songs 'which came to be identified with the mid-20th century Civil Rights Movement.' And yet, as Skinner Sawyers notes, what is the promised land 'but something that is out of reach, something that beckons but remains forever maddeningly elusive?' In other words: something in the night.

However, for all Springsteen's clear-eyed awareness in other songs of the promised land's intangibility, 'The Promised Land' itself focuses on the singer's determination and faith that it can be reached.

Granted, in the opening verse, his situation is grim. He is 'Working all day in [his] daddy's garage/Driving all night chasing some mirage', and sometimes he feels 'so weak [he] just wants to explode' and 'take a knife and cut this pain from [his] heart'. It's hardly an ideal situation.

But the challenges he faces only make him stronger. Rather than avoiding it, he is 'heading straight into the storm', even though it's 'gonna be a twister to blow everything down/That ain't got the faith to stand its ground'. But if that existential twister is a dream-destroyer, it's also capable of blowing away 'the lies that leave you nothing but lost and brokenhearted'. As he tells his paramour, despite the howling dogs on Main Street, 'Pretty soon, little girl, I'm gonna take charge'.

The upbeat tempo of 'The Promised Land' mirrors the defiant nature of the lyrics. Springsteen plays an abbreviated version of the melody on harmonica, and the band are right with him from the very start. Bittan's piano leads the way, but Springsteen and Van Zandt's guitars are more than present, and Federci's organ accents each important line.

After the second chorus, the piano and Springsteen's moaning come to the forefront. There's a touch of organ, then a brief guitar solo from Van Zandt, his first on a Springsteen record. Clemons follows with one of his three sax appearances on the album, and then Springsteen's harmonica takes a fuller turn with the melody. After the final verse and chorus, the harmonica wails the song's boldness all the way into the fadeout.

'Factory' (Springsteen)

At 2:30, the shortest song on the album, 'Factory', nevertheless makes a big impression. It's just three three-line verses followed by the tag, 'The working, the working, just the working life', but Springsteen conveys a great deal of information in those nine lines.

In the first stanza, we get a sharp visual picture of the initially unnamed protagonist's pre-work morning: getting out of bed early, dressing, grabbing his lunch (presumably prepared by his wife), then walking out into the early morning.

The second stanza begins by emphasizing the larger hold industrial work has on its workers – they must pass through 'mansions of fear' and 'mansions of pain' – then it zeroes in on his father, 'walking them factory gates in the rain', where the factory may give him life, but it also takes his hearing.

After a short keyboard break, things turn much grimmer: 'Men walking through these gates with death in their eyes'. Furious at the backbreaking work they must do in order to earn a living, and unable to take it out on the men who employ them, the workers are primed to retaliate on others of their own class: 'And you just better believe, boy/Somebody's gonna get hurt tonight'.

In a 1981 interview with Dave Marsh for *Musician* magazine, Springsteen explained the song's direct autobiographical relevance: 'There are people that get the chance to do the kind of work that changes the world and makes things really different. And then there's the kind that just keeps things from falling apart. And that was the kind my dad always did.'

It's ironic – or maybe appropriate – that Springsteen, who has often said he's never done much 'real' work outside of playing music, has, through his music, had the opportunity to 'make things really different' for many people, even if he hasn't quite changed the world. And he has done so by writing about people like his father, who have toiled and sweated in the sort of jobs Springsteen was never willing to do himself.

The song also benefits from its simple yet memorable three-chord melody. The piano and organ riff distantly echo 'I Don't Know How To Love Him' from *Jesus Christ Superstar*, a musical nod to the difficulty Springsteen and his father always had in expressing their feelings for one another, and a hint at the symbolic death of entering the factory and resurrection upon leaving its gates.

'Streets Of Fire' (Springsteen)

In *Springsteen Song By Song*, Clinton Heylin, alluding to the fact that 'Streets Of Fire' is one of the two earliest songs (along with 'Badlands') recorded for *Darkness*, suggests that 'It is certainly the least fully-conceived song on the album. Which doesn't make the song a total failure. In fact, it sounds like the spark that ignited the process.'

'Streets Of Fire' begins with Springsteen singing over Federici's solo organ for 50 seconds, right up to the chorus, which is simply the title sung four times. The full band kick in for the chorus, then settle down somewhat for the second verse. Halfway through, Springsteen's singing becomes louder, angrier, almost out of control, and then when the band heat up again for the second chorus, you can practically hear his throat burning as he draws out the word 'fire'.

Springsteen's guitar solo is as gnarly and guttural as his vocal stylings. He bends the strings of his Fender as though he wants to break them before the organ and piano join in, and then the instrumentation quiets down as the narrator acknowledges in the final verse that he lives and talks now 'only with strangers', and that even the angels he walks with 'have no place' in a world where he is 'strung out on the wire'. In the background, Tallent's bass marks time like a clock ticking towards doomsday.

Heylin calls the song 'A miniature noir movie, or indeed a noir trailer ... all sound and fury, thunder and lightning', and it's true that the angry lyrics aren't nearly as fully developed as, say, the title track or 'Racing In The Street'. Nevertheless, each verse presents a picture of the loneliness and anxiety the singer faces on a daily basis: 'The weak lies and the cold walls you embrace/ Eat at your insides'. And even when you think someone is calling your name in the darkness, it turns out to be a trick, 'all lies'.

'Prove It All Night' (Springsteen)

There's a seven-page spread in *Songs* showing the evolution of 'Prove It All Night' from one manuscript draft to the next. It's a bit chaotic, but you can see how meticulous Springsteen was in crafting every word. On one page, for instance, in the third verse, he writes, 'you can hear the(ir) voices' – he's still deciding which sounds better: 'the' or 'their'. ('Their', as it turned out.) In the next line, he originally wrote both 'baby' and 'girl' in the line 'Well they made their choices'. Ultimately, both words were crossed out. On and on it goes, and you quickly get a deeper appreciation for Springsteen's ability to make his music sound so spontaneous and raw when, in fact, it is so carefully planned.

If you were to look only at the chorus, which is mostly variations on the title, you might think that 'Prove It All Night' was simply another song in which a man is bragging about how he is going to have sex with his lover all night long. And, in some respects, that message is at the core of the track. But the real work of the song, as in so many of Springsteen's compositions on *Darkness*, comes in the verses.

In the first verse, with the band rocking out, we meet our archetypal working-class friend who loves driving his car with his girl, in this case, 'from Monroe to Angeline' so that he can buy her 'a gold ring and a pretty dress of blue'. In the second verse, the 'hunger' that people 'can't resist' is expanded from love and sex to something bigger, a dream that might or might not come true. But the only way to achieve it is to 'pay the price'.

We're left to think about that for a while during the instrumental break, during which Clemons's sax bleeds into Springsteen's guitar solo. Suddenly, with just a quiet drum and piano accompaniment, things have become much darker and riskier. The good-time couple of verse one has vanished, and now the singer is imploring his beloved to tie her 'hair back in a long white bow' and meet him 'in the fields out behind the dynamo'. It sounds more like the setting for a murder than a romantic rendezvous. And the singer has gone from a carefree potential fiancé to a man who seems angry at the world. There are no pretty blue dresses in the final verse: the singer is now chastising those who will 'never know/What it means to steal, to cheat, to lie/ What it's like to live and die'.

Nice bait and switch, you can almost imagine the young woman thinking, but Springsteen sings the song with such passion, and the E Street Band can make even the most ridiculous argument sound plausible, so it's hard not to ignore the song's dark turn and simply sing along with the catchy chorus.

'Darkness On The Edge Of Town' (Springsteen)

A great album needs a great closing song, and the title track of *Darkness On The Edge Of Town* meets that test. As Skinner Sawyers writes in *Tougher Than The Rest*, 'Everything on *Darkness* leads up to this snarling, bitter powerhouse of a ballad, a simmering fusion of angst and despair'. It is that, yes, but the song is also one of great resolve and even triumph.

The first verse, which begins with some almost hopeful piano chords, is the story of two former lovers who have parted ways. While working-class men are 'still racing out at the Trestles', 'that blood it never burned in her veins'.

Rather than hanging out with the street racers, the woman has moved 'up' in the world to Fairview, where she has 'a style she's trying to maintain'. It sounds like a tenuous hold on upward mobility, but it has separated the woman from the singer. The split is emphasized in the second half of the verse, when the band kick in, and Springsteen's singing shifts from laconic to frenzied. In fact, his growl has something of the anger at mistreatment and class oppression that infused so much of the best punk rock. The narrator is still hoping his old flame will want to see him, but if she does, she will have to return to *his* turf, that 'spot out 'neath Abram's Bridge' in the 'darkness on the edge of town'.

The second verse, as often happens in a Springsteen song, pans out to take a wider view of the situation described in the first verse. Now we learn that 'everybody's got a secret, son/Something that they just can't face/Some folks spend their whole lives trying to keep it/They carry it with them every step that they take'. In the second half of the verse, Springsteen tells us that the great weight of those secrets ultimately requires the people keeping them to let them go or else be destroyed: 'Someday they just cut it loose/Cut it loose or let it drag 'em down'. If there had been any question, by this point, we know clearly that the darkness on the edge of down is both physical and metaphysical.

The instrumental passage begins with piano, and a few shouted 'Huh!'s from Springsteen, then a guitar solo follows, but it's a short one, as though he doesn't want to lose the momentum he's been building up.

The final verse opens with a generality about class disparity – 'Some folks are born into a good life/And other folks get it in anyway, anyhow' – but then the singer returns to the first-person, and we learn he has lost his money and his wife, although 'Them things don't seem to matter much to me now'. Is his wife the woman in the opening verse, or is she just another person who's left him behind? In a way, it doesn't matter: the stage is set for one final stand by the singer. This time, however, rather than offering to go "neath Abram's Bridge', he's headed up to a hill 'with every thing [he's] got'. And like the narrators of 'Badlands' and 'Prove It All Night', he knows, to quote 'Thunder Road', that 'the ride ain't free'. 'I'll be there', he sings ferociously, 'and I'll pay the cost/For wanting things that can only be found/In the darkness on the edge of town'.

After that explosion of passion, the song takes nearly a minute to reach its conclusion. There are a few wordless moans from the singer, but it's mostly just piano, bass and drums played to fade out, ultimately ending with the opening chords, as though the song exists in an endless ontological loop.

Springsteen sums up not just this song, but the entire world of the album in his autobiography: 'With the record's final verse, 'Tonight I'll be on that hill…', my characters stand unsure of their fate but dug in and committed. By the end of *Darkness*, I'd found my adult voice.'

Above: Bruce Springsteen playing his iconic Fender Telecaster/Esquire hybrid guitar at the Los Angeles Memorial Coliseum in September 1985. (*AP Photo/Lennox McLendon*)

Left: Springsteen's first album; the cover is based on a postcard Springsteen brought to the Columbia Records design team. (*Columbia*)

Right: Springsteen's second album, released in November 1973, just ten months after the first record. Cover photograph by David Gahr. (*Columbia*)

Right: A leather-jacketed Springsteen leaning against the shoulder of Clarence Clemons on the cover of his third album. Photo by Eric Meola. (*Columbia*)

Left: The cover sleeve of the 45-rpm single of 'Born To Run', backed with 'Meeting Across The River'. (*Columbia*)

Above: A slightly amazed Bruce Springsteen inspecting an advance copy of his first album in late 1972. (*Art Maillet*)

Below: Bruce Springsteen and the E Street Band, Oklahoma, 1975. L-R: Gary Tallent, Danny Federici, Clarence Clemons, Springsteen, Max Weinberg, Steven Van Zandt, Roy Bittan. (*Barbara Pyle*)

Above: Bruce Springsteen and a somewhat dazed Little Steven Van Zandt performing during the *Born To Run* tour, October 1975. (*Fin Costello*)

Below: Springsteen with producer, mentor and loyal friend Jon Landau, 1974. (*Jeff Albertson/Department of Special Collections and University Archives/W.E.B. Du Bois Library/University of Massachusetts, Amherst*)

Left: The cover of Springsteen's fourth album, shot by Frank Stefanko in the photographer's New Jersey home. (*Columbia*)

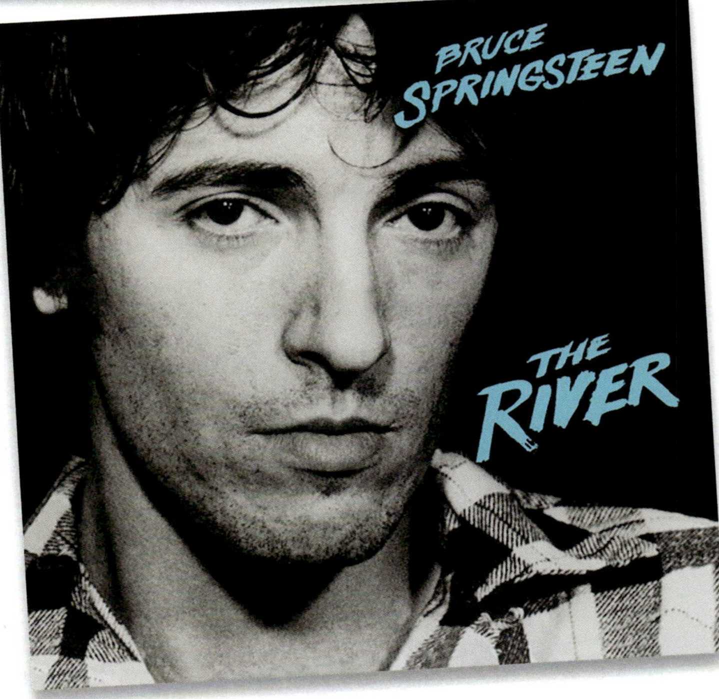

Right: The cover of Springsteen's fifth album, taken by Frank Stefanko during the same sessions as the *Darkness On The Edge Of Town* shoot. (*Columbia*)

Right: The record sleeve of Springsteen's first top ten hit, with the Boss standing near the Empress Hotel, Asbury Park, New Jersey. (*Columbia*)

Left: Springsteen's sixth album, with cover photo by David Michael Kennedy of a Colorado highway in December 1975. (*Columbia*)

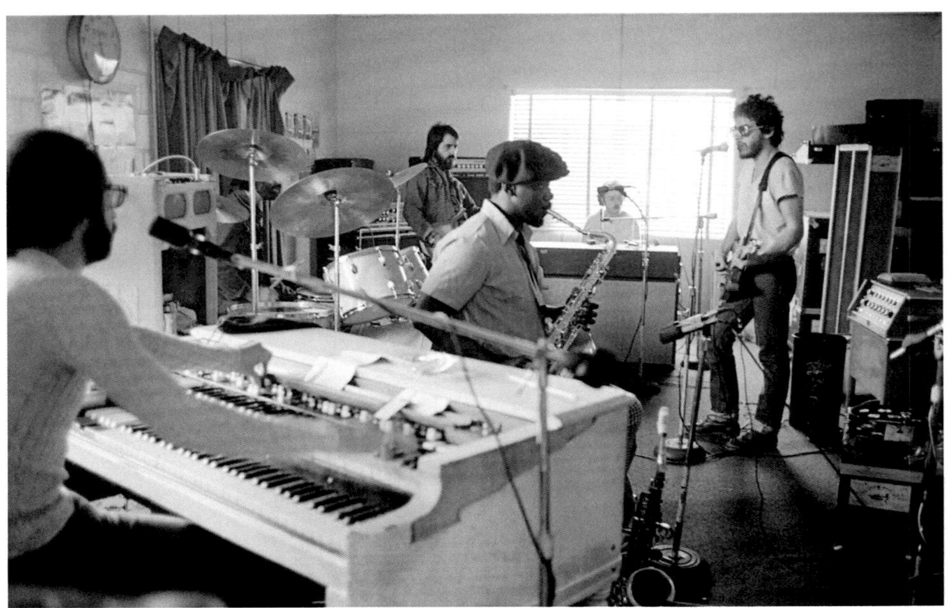

Above: Springsteen rehearsing with the E Street Band in Neptune, New Jersey, in 1975. L-R: Bittan, Weinberg (partially hidden by drums), Tallent, Clemons, Federici, Springsteen. (*Barbara Pyle/Reel Art Press*)

Below: A shot from the *Darkness On The Edge Of Town* tour, 1978. L-R: Clemons, Springsteen, Tallent. (Lynn Goldsmith)

Above: Van Zandt and Springsteen rehearsing material for *Darkness On The Edge Of Town* at Telegraph Hill Studio, Holmdale, New Jersey, 1978. (*Lynn Goldsmith*)

Below: *Darkness On The Edge Of Town* engineer Jimmy Iovine with Springsteen at a soundcheck in the Paramount Theater, Asbury Park, 1978. (*Lynn Goldsmith*)

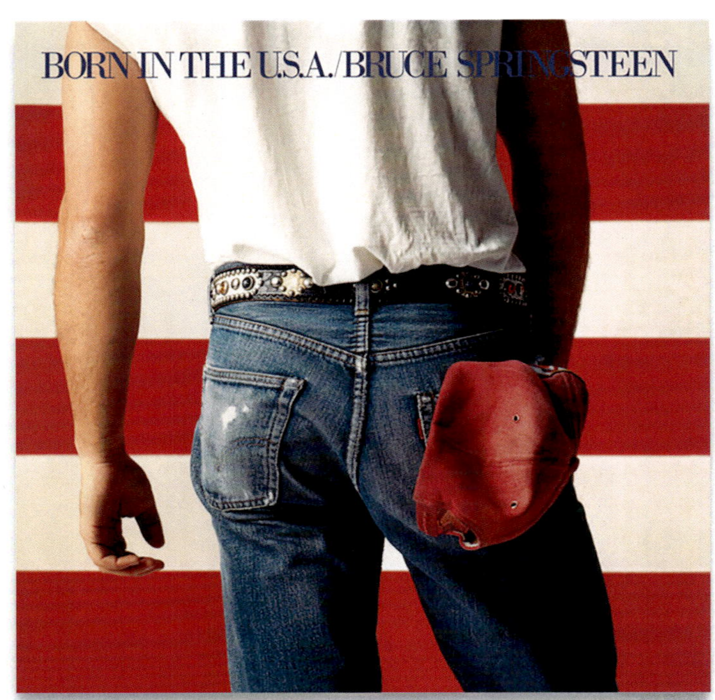

Left: *Born In The U.S.A.*, Springsteen's seventh and biggest-selling album. Cover photograph by Annie Leibovitz. (*Columbia*)

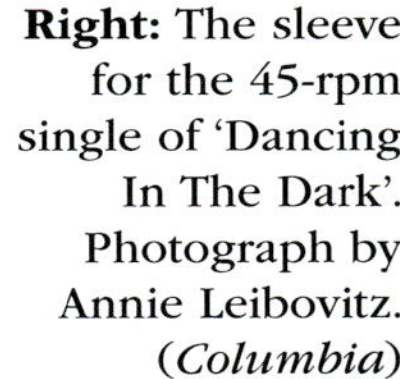

Right: The sleeve for the 45-rpm single of 'Dancing In The Dark'. Photograph by Annie Leibovitz. (*Columbia*)

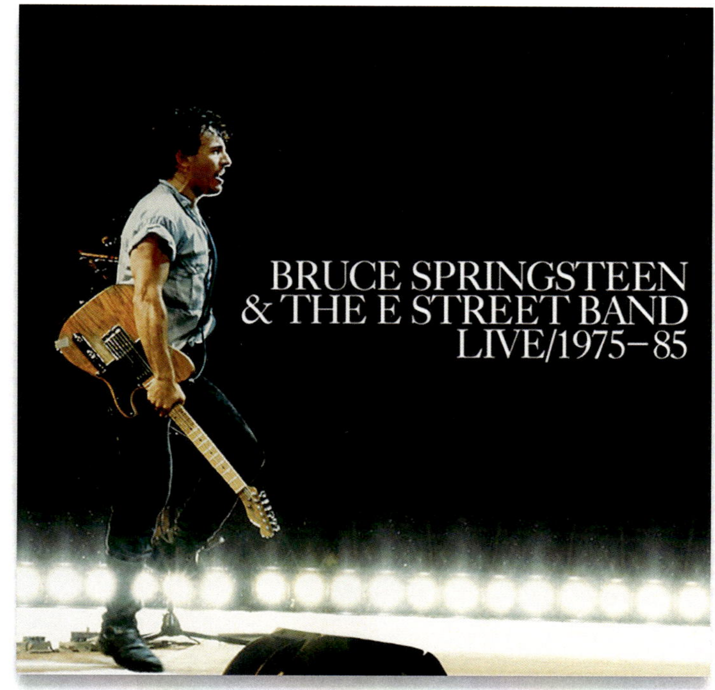

Right: The first of many live Springsteen albums. Cover photograph by Neal Preston. (*Columbia*)

Left: Springsteen's eighth studio album. Cover photograph of the new look Springsteen by Annie Leibovitz. (*Columbia*)

Left: The 'Dancing In The Dark' music video, directed by Brian De Palma, with the new E Street Band guitarist Nils Lofgren to Springsteen's right. (*Columbia*)

Right: A still from the 'Born In The U.S.A.' music video, directed by John Sayles.

Left: Max Weinberg, future leader of The Max Weinberg 7, the house band for *Late Night With Conan O'Brien*. (*Columbia*)

Right: A still from the music video for 'I'm On Fire', in which Springsteen plays an auto mechanic who lusts equally for a woman and her 1956 Ford Thunderbird. (*Columbia*)

Left: Springsteen at the wheel of the Thunderbird in 'I'm On Fire'. (*Columbia*)

Right: A still from the 'Brilliant Disguise' music video, shot as a single long take by director Meiert Avis. (*Columbia*)

Above: Clemons and Springsteen onstage in the early 1980s. (*Brooks Kraft LLC/Corbis via Getty Images*)

Right: Springsteen singing to his wife-to-be, Patty Scialfa, during the *Born In The U.S.A.* tour, Giants Stadium, 1985. (*AP Photo/ David Bookstaver*)

Above: Springsteen and Nils Lofgren in concert at Wembley Stadium, 1985. (*Steve Back/Rex/Shutterstock*)

Below: Springsteen performing during the *Tunnel Of Love* tour at Feijenoord Stadion, Rotterdam, 1988. (*Photo by Rob Verhorst/Redferns*)

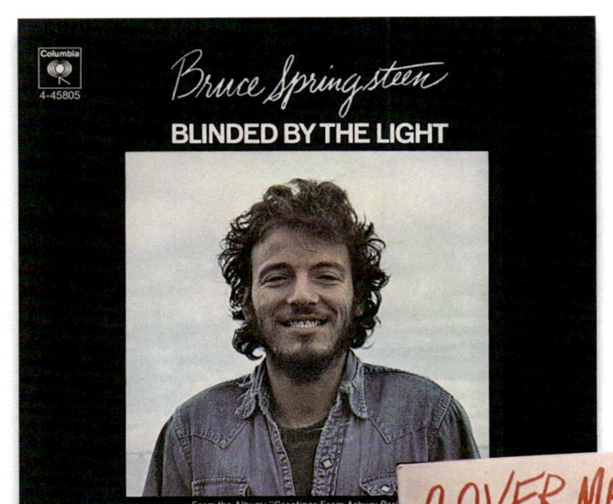

Left: The cover of a 45-rpm promotional single of 'Blinded By The Light' released in February 1973. Photograph by Fred Lombardi. (*Columbia*)

Right: Springsteen dressed for the mid-1980s on the cover of his second single from *Born In The U.S.A.*. Photograph by Annie Leibovitz. (*Columbia*)

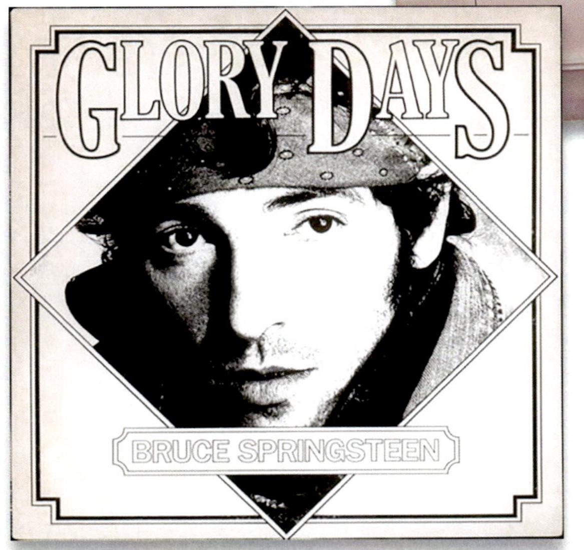

Left: The fifth of seven top ten singles from *Born In The U.S.A.*. Photograph by Aaron Rapoport. (*Columbia*)

The River (1980)

Personnel:

Bruce Springsteen: vocals, electric 6- and 12-string guitars, harmonica, piano on 'Drive All Night'

Roy Bittan: piano, organ on 'I'm A Rocker' and 'Drive All Night', background vocals

Clarence Clemons: saxophone, percussion, background vocals

Danny Federici: organ, glockenspiel on 'Hungry Heart'

Garry Tallent: bass guitar

Steve Van Zandt: acoustic and electric guitars, lead guitar on 'Crush On You', harmony vocals, background vocals

Max Weinberg: drums

Flo & Eddie (Howard Kaylan and Mark Volman): background vocals on 'Hungry Heart'

Recorded at Power Station, New York City, between March 1979 and August 1980

Producers: Bruce Springsteen, Jon Landau and Steven Van Zandt

Release date: 17 October 1980

Running time: 82:58

Label: Columbia

Album charts: US: 1, UK: 2

Singles charts: 'Hungry Heart' (US: 5, UK: 44), 'Fade Away' (US: 20), 'The River' (UK: 35)

'By the time *The River* came around,' Springsteen told Jann Wenner in a *Rolling Stone* interview, 'I knew a couple of things. I knew I wanted to include music that was just fun and exciting. I wanted that to be a part of what I was doing, the full range of my catalogue. I also wanted to keep my lyrical and conceptual intensity.' He amplifies these goals in his autobiography: '*The River* would be my first album where love, marriage and family would cautiously move to center stage.' He adds: 'After some time recording, we prepared a single album and handed it to the record company.'

That single album is a good place to begin a discussion of *The River*. Entitled *The Ties That Bind*, it was mixed by Bob Clearmountain to radio-friendly perfection at New York's Power Station recording studio in 1979. It's interesting to think about how the release of *The Ties That Bind* might have affected Springsteen's reputation among both fans and critics. (You can listen to the album, along with a couple of dozen outtakes, on 2015's *The Ties That Bind: The River Collection*.) There are three songs among the ten that didn't find their way to *The River*: 'Cindy', 'Be True' and 'Loose Ends'. The latter two have strong moments, but 'Cindy' is fairly insipid, with a plot line that could have been inspired by Dr. Hook & the Medicine Show's 'Sylvia's Mother'. The versions of the other songs, which fans have come to cherish, are generally more upbeat and tighter, but they lose the 'garage band' feeling that Springsteen admired and wanted, which is heard on this album. Oh, and 'You Can Look (But You Better Not Touch)' sounds like it was sung by an Elvis impersonator. Frankly, after the gut punch of *Darkness On The Edge Of Town*, the songs on *The Ties That Bind* sound a bit cheesy.

Fortunately, Springsteen recognized the problem. He writes in *Born To Run*: 'It sounded beautiful, but as I spent time listening to it, I felt it just wasn't enough.' What followed, as Springsteen describes it in his autobiography, was another year of working with the band and co-producers Jon Landau and Steven Van Zandt, along with 'mixmaster' Chuck Plotkin, rerecording, remixing and starting all over again: 'We needed to ruminate, contemplate, intellectualize and mentally masturbate ourselves into a paralytic frenzy.' It doesn't sound fun at all.

Fortunately, as ever, Springsteen had plenty of material to draw from. In addition to having the substantial backlog of unreleased songs from the *Darkness* years, he was continuing to write new work. In *Springsteen: Point Blank*, Christopher Sandford reckons that the band rehearsed or recorded nearly 90 songs during the two years of *The River*'s gestation period.

Finally, with the decision to move from a ten-song single-album to a 20-song double-album, Springsteen had enough room to achieve the combination of seriousness and fun he'd been seeking. Emotional depth came from ballads like 'Independence Day' and 'The River', while 'bar band' energy came from songs like 'Cadillac Ranch' and 'Ramrod'.

Yes, *The River* sometimes has the feeling of a miscellany – the clear through-lines of *Born To Run* and *Darkness* are much harder to find. But many of the great double-albums in rock 'n' roll history have a similar flavor, as though the artist's creativity couldn't be contained by a single style or theme. Think of Bob Dylan's *Blonde On Blonde*, The Beatles' *White Album*, Jimi Hendrix's *Electric Ladyland*, The Rolling Stones' *Exile On Main Street*, Elton John's *Goodbye Yellow Brick Road*, Led Zeppelin's *Physical Graffiti*, Stevie Wonder's *Songs In The Key Of Life*, The Clash's *London Calling* and Wilco's *Being There*. With its expansive and sympathetic view of working-class America, lyrics of both great depth and great fun, musical variety that ranges from straight-ahead rockers to achingly slow ballads and a mastery of the studio that makes it all sound of a piece, *The River* certainly belongs among that company.

The black and white front cover photograph was taken by Frank Stefanko at the same time as the *Darkness On The Edge Of Town* photo shoot. In a *Rolling Stone* interview with David Chiu, Stefanko recalls Springsteen had been looking through contact prints of that shoot, and he found one he liked: a 'close-up portrait shot, with the same plaid shirt that was in *Corvette Winter*', the title of the 1978 photograph on the cover of Springsteen's autobiography. Stefanko blacked out the background, which made room for Springsteen's name and the album title in a bright blue font.

The uncredited black and white photograph on the back cover looks like the odds and ends in the window of a rundown dime store. In front of a pegboard wall, five paper doll brides surround a single groom. Behind them is a 'Glow-Glitter' stick, a decal of an American eagle, a plastic American flag and a stack of paper cups. In the upper right-hand corner is a partial cutout of a bell – possibly the Liberty Bell? It's a kind of visual summation of the mix of songs found inside the album.

As usual, the critics (mostly) loved what they heard. Steve Pond wrote in the *Los Angeles Times*: 'At first, this simply sounds like Springsteen's party record, full of nods to Buddy Holly, Duane Eddy and The Byrds, and far happier than the brooding, unsettling *Darkness On The Edge Of Town* … Later, the remarkable cohesion, consistency and depth emerge.'

Rolling Stone continued to be all-but-worshipful in responding to the Boss's work. Paul Nelson's praise was of the sort normally reserved for Nobel Prize authors: 'What makes *The River* really special is Bruce Springsteen's epic exploration of the second acts of American lives. Because he realizes that most of our todays are the tragicomic sum of a scattered series of yesterdays that had once hoped to become better tomorrows, he can fuse past and present, desire and destiny, laughter and longing, and have death or glory emerge as more than just another story.'

Although he gave the album an 'A-', Robert Christgau had his quibbles: 'All the standard objections apply. His beat is still clunky, his singing overwrought, his sense of significance shot through with Mazola Oil. He's too white and too male, though he's decent enough to wish he weren't; too unanalytic and fatalistic, though his eye is sharp as can be.' Yet Christgau praised 'the condensed songcraft' that 'makes this double album a model of condensation'. In sum, Springsteen 'elaborates a myth about the fate of the guys he grew up with that hits a lot of people where they live.'

'The Ties That Bind' (Springsteen)

The first song on the album and the title song of the original collection, *Darkness*-era 'The Ties That Bind' clearly had an emotional resonance for Springsteen. Throughout *The River*, Springsteen is seeking moments that document 'the need for community', as he says in Dave Marsh's *Glory Days*, while also remaining aware of 'the other side, the need to be alone.'

The song's title is originally from a Baptist hymn, 'Blest Be The Tie That Binds', written in 1782 by John Fawcett. The ties that bind in the hymn were centered, naturally, on Christian love, but the phrase has long since moved to the secular, and Springsteen uses it here to describe the connection with his beloved. She is someone whom he believes would benefit from community ('you can't forsake the ties that bind'), despite her evident desire for solitude ('all alone you wanna ride/You don't want nothing, don't need no one by your side').

While the song's narrator is speaking directly to a woman, it's clear from Springsteen's autobiography that he might as well be talking to himself. Lines like 'You're so afraid of being somebody's fool/Not walking tough, baby, not walking cool' clearly apply to the young man who had just turned 30 when

The River was released and was looking for a way to move beyond the rock star's endless parade of fun but meaningless flings toward someone with whom he could have a lasting relationship. That person is still a figment of his imagination at this time, but at least he was looking.

There is no piano, organ or glockenspiel – those defining instruments of the previous two albums – giving 'The Ties That Band' something of a retro-rock feel. Guitars, including a 12-string Fender Eclectic XII played by Springsteen, dominate the soundscape for most of the song, although Clemons's solo after the bridge – 'I'd rather feel the hurt inside/Yes, I would darling/Than know … the emptiness your heart must hide' – seems to blow away those aching lines and replace them with the hope that so often spills forth from the bell of his horn.

Only 'Hungry Heart' and 'The Ties That Bind' were recorded by Bob Clearmountain for *The River*. Both have the shine of radio songs, and it's odd that 'The Ties That Bind' wasn't released as a single, especially considering some of the misfired non-charting singles that *were* released from the album, including 'Sherry Darling' and 'Point Blank'.

'Sherry Darling' (Springsteen)

Another song from the burst of creativity Springsteen experienced between *Born To Run* and *Darkness*, 'Sherry Darling', with its raucous comic energy, would have been a poor fit for the previous album, but its placement as the second song on *The River* is important. 'Sherry Darling', perhaps the silliest song on *The River*, signals that the Boss intends to have fun and joke around – he's not going to be a Gloomy Gus on every single track.

'Sherry Darling' begins with what sounds like a crowd of 15 or 20 people clapping, then going 'Whoa!' before Clarence Clemons swoops in with his saxophone. There's some half-singing of 'Hey, hey, hey, what do you say, Sherry Darling', but it sounds like people missed their mark, and the whole atmosphere is one of chaos and merriment.

Springsteen jumps in and announces that 'Your Mamma's yapping in the back seat/Tell her to push over and move them big feet/Every Monday morning I gotta drive her down to the unemployment agency'. This new character singing is a million miles away from the introspective narrator of 'Racing In The Street' and 'Darkness On The Edge Of Town', and the story he tells is humorous, with people at 'the party' yelling encouragement. The singer would much rather be partying with his girl, or at least be out on the beach, but instead, 'there's a hot sun beating on the blacktop', and he's 'stuck in traffic down here on 53rd Street' (a nod, wonders psychology professor David Sherman, to The Ramones' '53rd and 3rd'?) Clearly, he's had enough: 'Baby', he tells Sherry at the end of the second verse, 'this car just ain't big enough for her and me'.

At the break, Clemons's saxophone plays above the party noise, and then Springsteen joins with a single-string solo that sounds very early-1960s. The bridge begins with the grandiloquent lines 'Well, let there be sunlight, let there be rain/Let my broken heart love again' before Springsteen returns to the street, with a final shout out to 'all the girls down at Sacred Heart/And all you operators back in the Park', as Clemons wails on his saxophone, the revelers continue their revels and the song slowly fades to silence.

'Jackson Cage' (Springsteen)

Jackson Township is a 15-minute drive down Route 9 from Springsteen's hometown of Freehold. Whether or not that's the Jackson of the song – Springsteen loves citing random town names from around the United States – is unclear, but Jackson, New Jersey, does seem like a place where a person could feel trapped in a cage.

'Jackson Cage' uses the first-, second- and third-person points of view, giving the song a panopticon feel. In the opening verse, we meet a woman living in a town that looks like 'the scenery in another man's play'. The character is a 'she', and the singer seems to be an omniscient narrator looking in on her unhappy life.

However, in the chorus, Springsteen seems to be addressing her directly: 'You're reminded every day/That you've been judged and handed life/Down in the Jackson Cage'. That form of address continues in the second verse, where the description of the protagonist's life sounds even more depressing: 'There's always just one more day/And it's always gonna be that way'. Indeed, the narrator can tell by the way she moves that she belongs to the Jackson Cage, a place, the second chorus tells us, where if you aren't tough enough, you will 'just do your time and fade away'.

The music accompanying the lyrics doesn't always feel like a good match. The opening hook, played on the Farfisa organ by Federici, could come from a mid-1960s pop song, and Springsteen's harmonica at the break doesn't mirror the gloomy lyrics. The beat throughout is bouncy, if not jaunty. 'Jackson Cage' doesn't have the 'cage-like' feel of so much of the music on *Darkness*, although the song is much closer in spirit to that album than the tracks that precede and follow it.

'Two Hearts' (Springsteen)

'Two Hearts' opens with a description of a woman who could be the protagonist of 'Jackson Cage', or of any number of Springsteen's songs. 'She's been hurt so bad said she'd never love again'. However, the singer has a pleasant surprise for her: 'Someday your crying, girl, will end/And you'll find once again/Two hearts are better than one'.

Dave Marsh uses the second verse and chorus from 'Two Hearts' as the epigraph for his book *Glory Days: Bruce Springsteen In The 1980s*, and you can see why, at least in terms of the verse, in which the singer swears off 'playing tough guy scenes', announcing, 'Someday these childish dreams must end/To become a man and grow up to dream again'. If one of the main themes of *The River* is getting older and more mature, these lines sum up the experience pretty well.

The problem with the song is the chorus, which, frankly, is kind of dumb. 'Two are better than one; because they have a good reward for their labor', we learn in Ecclesiastes 4:9, and versions on that idea have been cliché for a couple of thousand years. Clichés can certainly work in rock songs – what would popular music be without them? – but this one is compounded by 'Two hearts get the job done', which sounds like it could be an advertisement for a romantic hardware store.

Nevertheless, 'Two Hearts' is a fun song overall: upbeat and optimistic, what Paul Nelson calls in *Rolling Stone* words of encouragement from 'an exceptionally warmhearted but wary graduate of the street of hard knocks.' A nice change for the man who for so long had been fruitlessly chasing something in the night.

'Independence Day' (Springsteen)

The final song on side one of the original LP is one of Springsteen's best, though its solemnity is in marked contrast to everything that has come before. As June Skinner Sawyers points out in *Tougher Than The Rest*, the tempo is 'the same slow death knell that Springsteen used in 'Factory': inevitable, unavoidable and absolute.'

'Independence Day' begins and ends with a simple but beautiful theme played by Federci on the organ, with Springsteen doubling the lines on acoustic guitar. Throughout, Bittan's piano playing is subtle, haunting, extraordinary and the rhythm section of Tallent and Weinberg manage to walk the fine sonic line between folk music and the rock 'n' roll ballad.

On *Darkness*, songs about fathers portrayed them as angry in 'Adam Raised A Cain' and pitiable in 'Factory'. This song, too – written all the way back in 1976 – was originally meant for that album, though it offers a different and deeper take on the father-son relationship.

The story begins *in media res*, at night, with the singer acknowledging to his 'papa' not only that 'Nothing we can say is gonna change anything now', but 'We wouldn't change this thing even if we could somehow'. They are sundered by fate, and acknowledging that fact and going their separate ways is the only path to avoid continually tormenting one another.

The 'Independence Day' being marked here is the parting of a father and son who 'were too much of the same kind', though it's odd that Springsteen didn't include any 4th of July imagery. After Clemons's moving sax solo in the instrumental break, Springsteen opens up the perspective to include images of Frankie's Joint and Breaker's Point, yet both of these locales are deserted – a strange phenomenon on a day noted for its rowdy celebrations.

But that's a small gripe with a song that manages to make the personal feel universal. And even as the two men part company, there's a suggestion of class solidarity in the final verse, when the singer announces that their small blue-collar world is on the verge of being utterly transformed: 'There's just different people coming down here now/And they see things in different ways/And soon everything we've known will just be swept away'.

'Hungry Heart' (Springsteen)

A friend recently said to me as we sat in a restaurant listening to the music on the P.A., 'That's a really bad cover of a Springsteen song.' Unfortunately, I had to break the news to her: 'I'm afraid that's the original.'

Bruce Springsteen's first top-five single, and, after 'Dancing In The Dark', his second-highest charting song (tied with 'Glory Days' and 'Brilliant Disguise'), is a bit of an odd duck for the Boss. Most prominently, Springsteen's voice was originally recorded at a slower tape speed, then sped up in the final version. Springsteen has said in interviews that the vocal made him sound 'like a chipmunk', but there was something about the higher pitch that appealed to casual radio listeners, many of whom had probably never heard a Springsteen record before.

Then there's the fact that Springsteen wrote the song for the great punk band The Ramones. As Rob Kirkpatrick points out in *Magic In The Night*, the song 'would have been an odd topic for the group, yet the surprisingly catchy, pop-friendly, roller-rink melodies of the song, not to mention its concise stanzas and uncharacteristic brevity, would have been well-suited' for the band.

Another unusual feature for a Springsteen song is the sweeping harmony vocals provided by Mark Volman and Howard Kaylan, aka Flo & Eddie, aka The Turtles of 'Happy Together' fame. In a 2013 interview with *Rock Cellar* magazine, Kaylan said of 'Hungry Heart': 'We just felt like [Springsteen] was wasting his time and we thought it was a throwaway bullshit B-side.' When the song came out and became one of the Boss's signature hits, Kaylan was not pleased, speculating: "We killed him, we ruined his career, this is horrible.' I loved the guy and now he put out this piece of crap.'

Still, for all its weirdnesses, 'Hungry Heart', driven by piano, organ and sax, and with only two verses but four variations on the chorus, does have a kind of timeless early rock 'n' roll feel: it might well have been a hit in the 1950s or 1960s, although it probably wouldn't chart today.

'Out In The Street' (Springsteen)

In a 1982 interview with *Modern Drummer* magazine, Max Weinberg calls his performance on 'Out In The Street' 'one of the worst bits of drumming I've ever done.' And yet, if his snare hits are just a fraction of a second too late, they give the song a punky flair that helps make the song feel authentically of 'the street'.

The story is a familiar one: the singer invites his best girl for a weekend night on the town, 'Way down beneath the neon lights'. They both deserve the break. 'All day [she's] been working that hard line', while he works 'five days a week/Loading crates down on the dock'.

With a nod to The Easybeats' 'Friday On My Mind', 'Out In The Street' celebrates the freedom of being off the clock. It's different from songs like 'Night' on *Born To Run* and 'Something In The Night' and 'Racing In The Street' on *Darkness* in that, rather than getting in his hot rod and heading out into blackness, he's actually socializing with his girl and their friends. 'In the crowd I feel at home' might seem like a throwaway line, but it's a big step forward from Springsteen's typically brooding narrators.

Musically, other than Weinberg's drumming, what's most notable about the song, which includes all the members of the E Street Band playing their assigned parts, is Clemons's sax solo, which is in two parts. The first two lines have the guitar following note for note when Clemons ends his run, then sax and guitar join together to finish out the solo.

The title is repeated too often at the end, but, with the lively music and notes of rebellion – 'We ain't gonna take what they're handing out' – the song is a solid entry in the Boss's catalog.

'Crush On You' (Springsteen)

Most definitely in the 'fun bar band' category, 'Crush On You' features Springsteen snarling over-the-top lyrics about the sexiness of his current crush. When he first sees her in someone else's car on the boulevard, he's so attracted to her that he wants 'to hold the bumper and let her drag [him] down the street'.

In the second verse, we learn these crushes of the singers are frequent ('Sometimes I spot a little stranger standing 'cross the room'), and therefore temporary. And in the extended final verse, we appear to return to his current object of desire, a fascination that is almost entirely physical. She may have 'a lousy personality', but 'She makes the Venus de Milo look like she's got no style/She makes Sheena of the Jungle look meek and mild'. Sheena is a character from the comic books of Springsteen's childhood, which makes the song feel somewhat dated, but his point is clear: when his libido is aroused, watch out!

The chorus is mostly just the title, with Van Zandt crooning 'Aw aw aw' after the first two lines, a strangely effective hook. The band are all in on the fun, and Clemons's solo, supported by some whooping and shouting from his bandmates, cements 'Crush On You' as another of Springsteen's three-chord party classics.

'You Can Look (But You Better Not Touch)' (Springsteen)

'There's a feeling of spontaneous combustion', Don McLeese wrote in *Racing In The Street: The Bruce Springsteen Reader* of songs on *The River* like this one, with 'sparks of influence from countless one-shot supernovas from our collective subconscious. Less Kierkegaard, lots more Kingsmen and Bobby Fuller.'

There is, of course, a point where you may have too much Kingsmen – the band that brought us 'Louie Louie' – and not enough Kierkegaard, and 'You

Can Look (But You'd Better Not Touch)' probably marks that moment in *The River*. Granted, the song has a fun guitar part, played by Springsteen, and the conceit is very straightforward – it's all in the title. The three examples of things you can look at but not touch are comic: a lamp at the mall, a pretty anchorwoman on the TV news and Dirty Annie, a character in the song.

And yet, let's be honest, like 'Sherry Darling' and 'Two Hearts' and 'Hungry Heart' and 'Crush On You', 'You Can Look (But You'd Better Not Touch)' is kind of silly, and, after the rock 'n' roll grandeur of the two previous albums, kind of disappointing for a certain type of 'serious' Springsteen fan.

Nevertheless, there's a sly allusion in the chorus when the Boss sings 'Mess around and you'll end up in Dutch'. Being 'in Dutch' is an oldfangled American idiom for being in trouble, but Dutch was also the nickname of Springsteen's father, and we can feel his disapproving patriarchal specter hovering over the song like a ghost.

'I Wanna Marry You' (Springsteen)

Springsteen's desire at this time to move fully into adulthood and possibly settle down is very much in evidence in 'I Wanna Marry You'. He sings the song with what feels like real sincerity, but the story in the song doesn't quite add up, which makes sense, as Springsteen has said in interviews that the idea for 'I Wanna Marry You' came to him in a dream.

The music itself has a dream-like quality, with Federci's organ, which could be in a church, or maybe a baseball game, filling the soundscape, as Tallent's bass lopes happily along, and Bittan adds piano flourishes. In the opening two verses, it seems clear that the singer does not know the woman he's addressing. Granted, he wonders if she has put 'that lonely ribbon' in her hair for him, but he's only seen her from afar, 'pushing that baby carriage', never smiling and, crucially, never speaking to her. 'Raising two kids alone in this mixed-up world', he muses, 'Must be a lonely life for a working girl'. Most likely it is, but he's a stranger: what business is it of his?

There is some discussion among fans about what the narrator means by 'working girl'. Is she a sex worker whom he sees, her two children in tow, coming back from a bordello every day? That seems unlikely. More believable is that she is a down-market version of the 'working girl' in the 1988 Harrison Ford-Melanie Griffith romantic comedy about an ambitious corporate secretary.

In any event, it seems peculiar that, as we learn from the chorus, the singer wants to marry someone he's never even met. The organ, which has dropped out after the introduction, returns, and things only get stranger in the second set of verses when the singer tells the woman, 'Now, honey, I don't want to clip your wings/But a time comes when two people should think of these things/Having a home and a family/Facing up to their responsibilities'. Certainly, the woman has an obligation to her two children, which she seems to be meeting, but what possible responsibilities does the singer have toward three people he's only seen from a distance? And does the woman have any say in this 'relationship' that seems to be entirely the projection of a man who's beginning to feel like something of a stalker? Or is he, as Springsteen said in a 1995 interview with Neil Strauss of *Guitar World*, 'just a guy standing on the corner fantasizing'?

In any case, backup singers, led by Van Zandt, join in the crooning as the narrator goes on to acknowledge that 'To say I'll make your dreams come true would be wrong/But maybe, darling, I could help them along'. The music and voices continue to swell as we reach the bridge, and we learn the narrator's father didn't believe in love and 'went to his grave a broken heart'. The singer sums it up: 'An unfulfilled life, girl, makes a man hard'. Maybe fear of that unfulfillment is why, in the final verse, he proposes to her: 'I'd be proud if you would wear my name'. Clemons solos on the tenor saxophone as the harmonies of the mostly unidentified background singers soar and Springsteen vamps his way to the fadeout.

'I didn't write about relationships', he said in the *Guitar World* interview about his early attempts to write songs like 'I Wanna Marry You', 'probably because I didn't know much about 'em, and I wasn't very good at 'em.' Indeed.

'The River' (Springsteen)

The final song on side two is another ballad and one of Springsteen's most stellar compositions, perhaps his greatest. Coming after the creepy-ish 'I Wanna Marry You', 'The River' feels like it was written by a different person altogether, which is either a tribute to Springsteen's versatility, or a reminder that even the best songwriters don't always hit it out of the park.

Like 'Thunder Road', 'The River' begins with a brief but poignant harmonica solo, although this one is played over an acoustic guitar rather than a piano. There's a slight echo on the guitar, but Springsteen's voice is plaintive, as he tells us that he comes 'from down in the valley/Where, mister, when you're young/They bring you up to do like your daddy done'. He tells us he met Mary when they were in high school, and they used to 'ride out of this valley/Down to where the fields were green'. While the Mary of 'Thunder Road' was told by the narrator that they were going to leave their 'town full of losers', it's not hard to imagine that, in fact, they didn't get very far, and this is the same young woman, or a version thereof.

Of course, the name Mary pops up often enough in Springsteen's Catholic-inflected work, and it doesn't much matter if this is the one we met on *Born To Run* because the real story is about what happens *after* the bass, drums and piano kick in on the chorus, and we reach the devastating second verse:

Then I got Mary pregnant
And, man, that was all she wrote
And for my nineteenth birthday
I got a union card and a wedding coat
We went down to the courthouse

And the judge put it all to rest
No wedding day smiles no walk down the aisle
No flowers no wedding dress

I quote this verse in full because it contains some of Springsteen's best writing. The first line is unsettling, and the second line, despite the cliché, slams shut the door of further possibility for the singer and his bride-to-be. The fact that he has to start working a union job at 19 essentially means he will never go to college, never leave the valley. His other nuptial present, 'a wedding coat', rather than a jacket or suit, tells us just how utilitarian this marriage is. And it only gets more dismal in the final four lines. There's no celebration here, simply the judge putting 'it all to rest', as though he were pronouncing a death sentence. No one but the couple seems to be at the civil ceremony – perhaps their families are too ashamed to make a big to-do, or else they just don't care.

That night, the couple go down to the river for the second time in the song. Less than a minute earlier, they were young and carefree as they dove into the water; now that diving feels like a futile attempt to escape from reality.

The harmonica returns for a full verse, bringing home the melancholy situation, and then we're into the final two verses. First, we learn that while the narrator 'got a job working construction.../lately there ain't been much work on account of the economy'. Meanwhile, as the singer acts like he doesn't remember their early courtship, 'Mary acts like she don't care'. And yet, in the last verse, the narrator can't help but recall those brief high school moments when he and his now-wife were happy: 'those memories come back to haunt me, they haunt me like a curse'. Then he asks the fateful question: 'Is a dream a lie if it don't come true/Or is it something worse/That sends me down to the river', which we learn is now dry.

Springsteen says in his autobiography that he got the idea for 'The River' after listening to a very different song, Hank Williams's comic 'My Bucket's Got A Hole In It'. Then, 'I drove home to New Jersey and sat at a small oak table in my bedroom, watching the dawn sky draw blue out of the black, and I imagined my story. It was a guy in a bar talking to the stranger on the next stool.'

In fact, the story very closely follows the life of his sister, Ginny, and brother-in-law, Mickey, and despite the pain it reveals, she has expressed satisfaction at having part of her life told in such poignant terms. In the end, of course, the song speaks to anyone who has found themselves trapped in an unhappy relationship, which may explain its lasting resonance for so many listeners.

'Point Blank' (Springsteen)
If Springsteen was catering to casual fans with sing-along party songs like 'Hungry Heart' and 'Crush On You', 'Point Blank' shows that he still wasn't

afraid to make bold artistic moves. The first song on the second LP of a double-album was often the place for a rocker. Think of 'Birthday' on The Beatles' *White Album*, or 'Happy' on The Rolling Stones' *Exile On Main Street*.

Springsteen goes in the opposite direction. 'Point Blank' is a six-minute ballad led by Bittan's piano playing and Tallent's smart, subtly funky bassline. Federci's Hammond B-3 organ also has an important role, as do Van Zandt's harmony vocals on the chorus, which adds a note of anguish to Springsteen's gloomy lyrics.

Those lyrics tell the tale of another of Springsteen's downcast female characters who are doing their best, despite being dealt a lousy hand by Fate. This particular woman, we learn at the end of the first verse, wakes up and is 'dying/[She] don't even know what from'. The problem, it turns out, is that she's been shot 'point blank.../Right between the eyes'. Clearly, the shooting is metaphorical, but its effects on her seem to have been physically painful, in addition to the emotional damage she has suffered.

The villain of the piece is unnamed. Partly, to be sure, it's her environment: 'You grew up where young girls they grow up fast/You took what you were handed and left behind what was asked'. Whatever has happened, the woman, whom the singer once thought of as Juliet to his Romeo, no longer waits on Romeo. Instead, he sings, 'You wait on that welfare check/And on all the pretty little things that you can never have/And all the promises that always end up point blank/Shot between the eyes'.

The long final verse begins with a dream the speaker has had, a romantic memory of the woman at a club when they were young. But in reality, she seems to have fallen even further than in the previous verse: 'Well, I saw you last night down on the avenue/Your face was in the shadows but I knew that it was you'. She doesn't answer when he calls her name, and he now views her as 'just another stranger, waiting to get blown away'.

'Cadillac Ranch' (Springsteen)

On two sides of the lyric sheet included with the original vinyl album, we see black and white photographs of Cadillacs half-buried in the dirt: they look like they've crashed down from the sky. This is the Cadillac Ranch, a public art installation just west of Amarillo, Texas, that was created in 1974 by Chip Lord, Hudson Marquez, and Doug Michels.

The Springsteen version of 'Cadillac Ranch' is a rockabilly number drawing on the whimsy of the installation. It's an imaginary place, both good – the narrator is going to pack up his pa and his aunt and take them there – but also a kind of graveyard. 'Don't let 'em take me to the Cadillac Ranch', he says in the final verse. Ultimately, the Cadillac Ranch seems to be a place where Cadillacs and hot rods of all sorts – like those driven by James Dean, Junior Johnson (a 1950s racecar driver) and movie star Burt Reynolds – all meet up. One might even say that the title is mostly an excuse to sing the word 'Cadillac', which appears ten times in the song.

'Cadillac Ranch' is just three minutes long, but the singing doesn't begin until half a minute in, as the Boss's rockabilly guitar riff is joined by Bittan's rockabilly piano. They generate a lively rhythm, so that it doesn't much matter what the lyrics are as long as we understand that the car of choice for 1950s rockers is 'Long and dark, shiny and black', and when its engines are roaring, you'll find it 'Tearing up the highway like a big old dinosaur'.

'I'm A Rocker' (Springsteen)

There is something undeniably ballsy about the heavy repetition in 'I'm A Rocker'. Bittan plays the same trebly piano riff, ad nauseam, throughout the song, and Van Zandt, Bittan and Clemons sing 'I'm a rocker, baby, I'm a rocker' so many times you may never want to hear the phrase again.

The premise of the verse is funny enough. When it comes to taking care of his baby's love, the singer is even better than a spy (007 and the agents on *Mission Impossible*), a superhero (Batman) or a TV cop (Columbo or Kojak). However, as with a number of cultural references throughout Springsteen's work, these feel a bit passé. *Kojak* had been off the air for a couple of years by the time *The River* was released, and the *Batman* TV series ended in 1968. Then there's the apparent reference to even cornier material, with 'If you're hanging from a cliff or you're tied to the tracks, girl'. If that latter image doesn't evoke Snidely Whiplash of *The Rocky And Bullwinkle Show*, it's something equally silly.

The song doesn't quite hang together. Being a rocker is different from being a spy or superhero or a cop. And yet, similar to a runaway train barreling toward that girl tied to the tracks, 'I'm A Rocker' hurtles forward, with the E Street Band stoking the engine, and the Boss with his hand on the throttle, full speed ahead.

'Fade Away' (Springsteen)

Considering how many up-tempo songs there are that might have followed 'Hungry Heart' as the album's second single, 'Fade Away' doesn't seem like an obvious choice. But June Skinner Sawyers is right: 'Pain has never sounded so gorgeous. Springsteen's forlorn ballad of lost love and one man's desperate attempt to regain what he once had is a great song, one of the best on *The River*.'

The song begins with both pianist and organist playing their hearts out. There's more than a touch of gospel in the mix as Springsteen tells us, like millions of men before and after, that he can't believe his sweetheart has found 'another man who does things to you' that he can't, and that she is no longer in love with him. In the chorus, he asks, 'What can I do? What can I say?', but one has the feeling that at this late stage of the relationship, the answer is probably 'Nothing'.

As usual, Tallent's bass manages to bring out the most interesting aspects of a fairly standard chord structure, but it is Federici's B-3 solos that sum up the singer's angst. By his own admission, the narrator has let slide the little things that might have kept his lover interested in him, like a night on the town, dancing and having fun. Nevertheless, he tells her he doesn't want to end up being 'just some other ghost out on the street/To whom you stop and politely speak', but that, both the sorrowful music and the grief-stricken singing tell us, is exactly what he will become.

The fact that the melancholy 'Fade Away' managed to hit the number 20 spot on the *Billboard* Hot 100 during the week of 14 March 1981, when other top 20 hits included Dolly Parton's '9 To 5', REO Speedwagon's 'Keep On Loving You' and Kool & the Gang's 'Celebration', is a testament to the passion Springsteen and the entire band put into the recording.

'Stolen Car' (Springsteen)

One of the great two-chord songs in the rock 'n' roll canon, 'Stolen Car', Springsteen tells us in *Songs*, 'was the predecessor for a good deal of the music I'd be writing in the future. It was inner-directed, psychological; this was the character whose progress I'd soon be following on *Tunnel Of Love*. He was the archetype for the male role in my later songs about men and women.'

Those are some big claims for a song consisting of three four-line verses and a chorus, but there is something especially poignant about the song. The spare nature of the lyrics and music emphasizes the speaker's loneliness. Especially in comparison to the earlier version of the song found on *Tracks*, *The River*'s 'Stolen Car' achieves a luminosity through the philosophy of less-is-more.

The story is another of Springsteen's tales of love gone wrong: this particular couple have 'settled down/In a little house on the edge of town'. We know from the previous album that there's darkness in such places, so it's not surprising that by the second stanza, the couple are already breaking up. The narrator finds himself driving a stolen car in the first chorus: 'Each night I wait to get caught/But I never do'.

The next verse offers a sad but sympathetic portrait of the narrator's lost love. She asks him if he remembers the letters he wrote when their love 'was young and bold'. Her follow-up is heartbreaking: 'she read those letters last night/And they made her feel one hundred years old'. And so, in the second and final chorus, the singer is no longer worried about getting caught. Now, he's in an existential crisis, in the 'pitch black' night in which he drives: 'I travel in fear/That in this darkness I will disappear'.

Springsteen's desolate singing is accompanied by his heavily reverbed acoustic guitar. Weinberg's quiet and subtle drumming on the toms provides a steady rhythm for Tallent's moody bass, Bittan's mournful piano and Federici's ever-evocative Hammond organ.

'Ramrod' (Springsteen)

The first song on the final side of the double album is another rocker. The word 'ramrod' comes from the 17th century and was a rod used to pack powder and a projectile into a firearm. In contemporary usage, to ramrod something is to 'force a proposed measure to be accepted or completed quickly'. That 'proposed measure' can include forced sex, although that doesn't appear to be the case here. *Ramrod* is also a 1947 Western movie, in which the word is used to refer to a ranch foreman.

Most germanely, a ramrod is another word for a stick shift in a manual transmission car, and for Springsteen the word seems to connotate both fast cars and fast women: 'Hey little dolly, with the blue jeans on/I want to ramrod with you, honey, till half-past dawn'. For the singer, a fast car and a good-looking paramour almost seem to be one and the same. He seeks out his car, 'a hot stepping hemi with a four on the floor', like a hot date: 'Come Saturday night I let my ramrod rock'. He also tells us that 'Late at night when I'm dead on the line/I swear I think of your pretty face when I let [my car] unwind'.

In an interview with Dave Marsh, Springsteen said that he saw the song as 'sort of like a partner to 'Cadillac Ranch' ... it's got that old big engine sound'. In addition to churning guitars from Springsteen and Van Zandt, Clemons plays throughout the track, playing a big, if brief, saxophone solo, with the whole band providing echoey handclaps in time with Weinberg's snare. Unfortunately, like 'I'm A Rocker', 'Ramrod' features an annoying repeated keyboard riff throughout the song, this time played on Federici's organ.

Happily, compared to the majority of the songs on sides three and four of *The River*, 'Ramrod' posits an optimistic ending for both the singer and the object of his eye. If she'll just meet the singer 'tonight up on top of the hill', she'll have a much better outcome than the singer of 'Darkness On The Edge Of Town'. In fact, if she hops into his fast car, he'll take her across the county line to 'a cute little chapel nestled down in the pines', where the two can be wed and then together 'go ramrodding forever more'.

'The Price You Pay' (Springsteen)

We know from 'Adam Raised A Cain' that 'You're born into this life paying/For the sins of somebody else's past', and from 'Prove It All Night' that if you really want something, you'd better be prepared to 'pay the price', and from 'Darkness On The Edge Of Town' that sometimes you have to 'pay the cost', so it's no surprise to have an entire song devoted to this subject.

In Chapter 34 of Deuteronomy, God takes Moses up to the top of Mount Nebo and shows him a great vista that includes the land of Gilead and Judah, 'unto the utmost sea'. It is, essentially, the promised land, but Moses has been disobedient and has not trusted God, and the result is dire. God says, 'I will give it unto thy seed: I have caused thee to see it with thine eyes, but thou shalt not go over'.

Springsteen recounts a version of this story in the fourth verse of 'The Price You Pay'. Things seem dire for us, the listeners, who have been addressed as 'You' earlier in the song. We've been told in the first verse that we're going to have to go out on the open road and 'ride until the day/You learn to sleep at night with the price you pay'. Moreover, in the second verse, those of us who have 'reached out for the open skies' will likely have to drive on roads we've built ourselves until we ride to our own deaths. In the third verse, Springsteen refers to people who have 'come so far and … waited so long/[But] just end up caught in a dream where everything goes wrong'. The chorus makes it plain: 'you can't walk away from the price you pay'.

And yet it's important to remember that Springsteen's 'story of the promised land' is addressed to a 'Little girl down on the strand/With that pretty little baby in your hands'. For all its pessimism, the song is about pushing back against the powerful entities that want to keep the common man and woman down. In the final verse, Springsteen announces, 'So let the game start, you better run, you little wild heart'. Things will be tough, he tells her and us, but when the authorities put up a sign announcing how many people 'have fallen away to the price you pay', the Boss will lead us on. He's going to take that sign and 'tear it down and throw it away'.

'The Price You Pay' has a slower tempo than 'The Promised Land', but they both enter with a big drum and piano sound and a steady beat that signals the momentum of the song will not be stopped. The earlier song begins with harmonica, but Springsteen doesn't play harp until the break, when he blows a Dylan-esque solo that's a perfect match for the song's mood. Right afterwards, with Tallent plucking single notes on the bass, Federici enters with his accordion, bringing back memories of the first two albums and the early E Street Band. Overall, it's a commanding musical performance, especially the outro, when Federici's accordion and Bittan's piano meet Weinberg's crashing cymbals in the long fade.

'Drive All Night' (Springsteen)

The same three chords played in the same progression for eight and a half minutes: it sounds like a composition by avant-garde composers Steve Reich or Philip Glass. In fact, this is the music for 'Drive All Night', and with variations in dynamics and accompaniment, those three chords don't sound nearly as monotonous as they might. In fact, the music provides Springsteen with the background for one of his greatest vocal performances.

We noted earlier that 'Drive All Night' had been the middle part of an extended live version of 'Backstreets', and on *The River*, it's possible to see why this was such a showstopper. The song, which begins with Tallent's bass, is agonizingly slow, but Springsteen brings everything he has to 'Drive All Night', making us feel as though driving all night to buy someone a pair of shoes and to 'taste [their] tender charms' is the height of romantic passion.

We know from dozens of other compositions that this songwriter likes to drive at night anyway, so maybe it's not such a big ask, but by the sixth minute, when he tells his beloved that she has his love, 'heart and soul', those three words sound like they represent the apex of human expression. As he wails them four times, his voice is strained and gravelly, yet emotionally pure.

'Drive All Night' continues another two minutes after that climax, with Van Zandt offering some lovely response vocals – 'Don't Cry Now' – and the energy of the song picks up again as Springsteen, like some crazed postman, says he will drive through the snow and wind and rain to deliver his love to his baby.

How does the Boss pull off this magic? Primarily, it's his literally breathtaking vocal performance, but the band are with him all the way. Bittan's piano never lets Springsteen down, and Clemmons's solo, nearly a minute long, is dreamy as hell – you feel like you could listen to it forever.

'Wreck On The Highway' (Springsteen)

How do you end an album as varied and ambitious as *The River*? The answer, Springsteen felt, was quiet introspection. In *Songs*, he says that 'Wreck On The Highway' is 'about confronting one's own death and stepping into the adult world where time is finite ... [Y]ou have a limited number of opportunities to love someone, to do your work, to be part of something, to parent your children, to do something good.'

The title is taken from Roy Acuff's 1942 song of the same name, and Springsteen even borrows some details, like the blood and glass on the asphalt. However, Acuff's song is decidedly more religious. His primary concern is that after the crash, 'I didn't hear nobody pray'.

Springsteen, in contrast, never mentions the destination of the soul of the man who has died 'in the drizzling rain/On a deserted stretch of a county two-lane'. Instead, he focuses on the people the man left behind: 'I thought of a girlfriend or a young wife/And a state trooper knocking in the middle of the night/To say your baby died in a wreck on the highway'. While it seems unlikely that a trooper would refer to the deceased as 'your baby', this mini-scene is evocative, topped only by the final stanza, which foreshadows the end of a lovely song on *Tunnel Of Love*, 'Cautious Man'.

While Springsteen's song is markedly different from Acuff's, his 'Wreck On The Highway', despite Federici's soulful organ fills, has a decidedly country flavor. It's probably closer to Johnny Cash's 'Give My Love To Rose', which also has a narrator recounting his meeting with a dying man. Without a doubt, both songs are landmarks, as is *The River* itself.

Bonus Tracks
'Held Up Without A Gun' (Springsteen)

B-side of 'Hungry Heart'
If ever a song were needed to prove that the Boss understood the angry heart of punk rock, this would be prime evidence. At a minute and 15 seconds, 'Held Up Without A Gun' is over almost before it's begun, but there's a lot of pent-up energy released in its brief time on the turntable.

Just before he begins singing, Springsteen yells, 'Come on, Steve!' and you can hear him and Van Zandt in what is practically a duet. The full band, including Clemons, are playing, but the muddy mix makes it all sound like one glorious batch of guitar-driven noise.

The lyric's premise is simple. In verse one, the singer is held up without a gun because the gas he is trying to buy is so expensive. In verse two, a naïve guitar player signs with a shady manager (Mike Appel?). And the final verse suggests how likely it is that *someone* will take advantage of us: 'Now it's a sin/And it oughta be a crime/You know it happens, buddy/All the time'.

Coming as it does on the back of the album's biggest hit, and one of its dumbest songs – 'this piece of crap', as backup singer Howard Kaylan called 'Hungry Heart' – the garage band-influenced 'Held Up Without A Gun' seems to be a statement to record buyers in 1980: Bruce Springsteen is a lot more than just a top 40 star.

'Be True' (Springsteen)
B-side of 'Fade Away' and 'Sherry Darling'
Prior to *The River*, Springsteen's B-sides were songs available on his albums, but beginning with 'Hungry Heart' and 'Fade Away', he began releasing some of his vast backlogged repertoire on the flip sides of his hits.

'Held Up Without A Gun' is a bit of a throwaway, but 'Be True' is a more fully developed song. The conceit is that the 'little girl' the singer is addressing is so caught up in the spectacle of watching motion pictures that she inevitably must settle for men who use her when she returns to real life: 'You see all the romantic movies/You dream and take the boys home/But when the action fades/You're left all alone'. The singer implores her not to 'end up just another lonely ticket sold/Cryin' alone in the theater as the credits roll'. His solution: 'Well, baby, you be true to me/And I'll be true to you'.

Springsteen's analogy is carefully wrought, and the music, mixed by Bob Clearmountain, is clean and full of punch. Piano and organ lead the way until the instrumental at the end. The song winds down with more than a minute of bluesy saxophone playing from Clemons and some soulful 'Yeah, yeah's from the Boss. This is a good one, and you can see why it was included on the original single-album version of *The River*.

Nebraska (1982)

Personnel:
Bruce Springsteen: vocals, guitars, harmonica (except 'State Trooper' and 'Open All Night'), mandolin ('Nebraska', 'Atlantic City', 'Mansion On The Hill' and 'Highway Patrolman'), glockenspiel ('Nebraska' and 'Used Cars'), synthesizer ('My Father's House')
Recorded at Springsteen's rented home in Colts Neck, New Jersey, between 17 December 1981 and 3 January 1982; 'My Father's House' on 25 May 1982
Producer: Mike Batlan (engineer)
Release date: 30 September 1982
Running time: 41:02
Label: Columbia
Album charts: US: 3, UK: 3

If Bruce Springsteen had gone down the folk path that his bosses at Columbia Records back in the early 1970s had wanted him to tread, *Nebraska* might not have caused the same stir. Granted, the album might have been seen as something of a walk-back. Listeners would probably have been happy that some of the rhyming dictionary excesses were gone from the lyrics, but musically, they would have been disappointed. There's a lot more going on in 'Blinded By The Light' and 'Spirit In The Night', and even 'Mary Queen Of Arkansas', than there is on any of the songs on *Nebraska*.

That's not to say the music, mostly provided by Springsteen's acoustic guitar and harmonica, isn't befitting of the lyrics. The spare quality of the imagery and storytelling throughout the album is matched by familiar chord patterns, straight out of early blues and classic folk and country songs. This is a world more intent on reporting than judging. As June Skinner Sawyers notes, 'Springsteen navigates moral gray areas using [Nebraska] and its flat, open, featureless landscape as an emotional shorthand for the bleak portraits of murderers, loners and other assorted misfits from the other side of Ronald Reagan's America. The moral here is that anybody can do anything: evil and good reside in the same person.'

In *Songs*, Springsteen recalls one of the impetuses for *Nebraska*: 'I'd grown tired of expending so much energy in professional recording studios where I rarely got the right group of songs I was after without wasting a lot of time and expense.' Springsteen 'found the atmosphere in the studio to be sterile and isolating, and the long, drifting records emotionally wearing. I decided I needed to find a way to hear my songs before I brought them into the studio.'

He picks up the story in *Born To Run*: 'I sent my guitar tech out to get a recorder, a little less lo-fi than the cassette record I usually used to lay down my new song ideas ... He came back with a four-track Japanese Tascam 144 cassette recorder.' With the two tracks left over after he had recorded his guitar and voice, Springsteen 'could add a backing vocal, an extra guitar or a tambourine.' The equipment was, in the words of Warren Zanes in *Deliver Me*

From Nowhere, 'the first major bid to establish a territory between studio-grade recording gear and the cassette recorders that kids played with.' With the addition of a guitar Echoplex unit for delay and reverb, the whole thing set Springsteen back less than $1000.

Springsteen's makeshift studio was a bedroom in the small house he was renting in Colts Neck, New Jersey. The carpeting was orange shag, and the lone window looked out on a small reservoir, rather desolate at the end of December 1981 and the beginning of January 1982, when most of the album was recorded. Mike Batlan, the guitar tech, was often in the room when Springsteen was recording, though the Boss preferred not to mention that fact. Batlan was also responsible for the basic mixing of the tracks, which he did on an old Panasonic boombox.

Rather than insisting that the full band hang around until dawn just in case he wanted to do the 20th recording of the same song, Springsteen now often settled for raw spontaneity. The perfectionist who had spent months and months on individual songs on his three previous albums was now signing off on tracks that had 'three, maybe four takes', as he writes in *Songs*. 'Some, like 'Highway Patrolman' and 'State Trooper', only one.' You can hear the minor mistakes – a fumbled chord, a misspoken word – but, like the 1960s albums of Bob Dylan, these errors make *Nebraska* feel fresh and blessedly unrehearsed.

Of course, details about the making of the album might not be so important if Springsteen weren't in the full-time business of mythmaking. Indeed, this period in his career, when he decided to buck the record company executives who wanted another big hit album rather than a collection of homemade country-folk songs, was so full of drama that they made a movie out of it – 2025's *Deliver Me From Nowhere*, based on Zanes's book, directed by Scott Cooper, and staring Jeremy Allen White as Springsteen.

Taking advantage of the hype surrounding the film, Springsteen put out an expanded version of the album the same month the movie was released. The box set includes a disc of outtakes – electric versions of six of the ten songs on the original album, played, in Springsteen's words, 'kinda like punk rockabilly', with just guitar, bass and drums – and a DVD of a live solo acoustic version of Springsteen performing the songs in 2025.

The original album's stark front cover has become iconic. A low-resolution black and white photograph, taken by David Michael Kennedy through the front window of his pickup truck, shows snow on the wiper blades and a straight black highway stretching out into flat empty distance, with barbed wire fences on both sides of the two-lane blacktop road. On top of the photo, in bright red full caps on a black background, is the artist's name. At the bottom is the album's title. The back cover simply lists the ten songs on the album in all caps in the same red font on the same black background.

Back in 1982, when the album was first released, it caught a number of fans off guard. Those who were partial to songs on *The River* like 'Cadillac Ranch' and 'I'm A Rocker' were generally not interested in the new material. Nevertheless, most critics were fairly quick to get on board with this sharp departure from the Boss's previous albums. *Time* magazine said *Nebraska* was 'an acoustic bypass through the American heartland ... like a Library of Congress field recording made out behind some shutdown auto plant.' Steve Pond in *Rolling Stone*, which was by now practically an extension of the Springsteen PR machine, raved: '*Nebraska* is an acoustic triumph, a basic folk album on which Springsteen has stripped his art down to the core. It's as harrowing as *Darkness On The Edge Of Town*, but more measured. Every small touch speaks volumes: the delicacy of the acoustic guitars, the blurred sting of the electric guitars, the spare, grim images.'

Like Charlie Starkweather, the narrator of 'Nebraska', Gary Gilmore, the brother of rock journalist Mikal, had been executed following conviction on multiple counts of murder. Mikal Gilmore could have had legitimate issues with the subject matter, but instead, in the *Los Angeles Times*, he called the album 'the most successful attempt at making a sizable statement about American life that popular music has yet produced'.

Granted, Robert Christgau had his usual reservations: 'the music is a problem here – unlike, er, Dylan, or Robert Johnson ... Springsteen isn't imaginative enough vocally or melodically to enrich these bitter tales of late capitalism with nothing but a guitar, a harmonica and a few brave arrangements. Still, this is a conceptual coup, especially since it's selling.' And sell the record did.

Even though it was a flop compared to *The River*, *Nebraska* – without a serious single – still reached number three on the album charts in both the US and UK, and quickly went gold.

'Nebraska' (Springsteen)

In *Songs*, Springsteen calls 'Nebraska' the 'record's center', and it has certainly garnered the sort of attention such a track might warrant.

Springsteen had long been fascinated by Terrance Malick's *Badlands* – it had been the inspiration for the title of the song on *Darkness* – but now he looked deeper into the story behind the film. In the movie, Sissy Spacek, as 15-year-old Holly, and Martin Sheen, as 25-year-old Kit, go on a killing spree after Kit murders her father, and they fake a suicide after burning down her house. For most of the rest of *Badlands*, they are on the run across the 'badlands' of South Dakota and Montana, with Kit murdering anyone who gets in their way.

Malick's script is based on the story of 19-year-old Charlie Starkweather and his 14-year-old girlfriend Caril Ann Fugate. Starkweather killed ten people in the span of eight days, and 11 people overall. Like Springsteen's song, Starkweather's murders took place in and around Lincoln, ultimately ending in his capture and arrest in Wyoming. The gruesome story was national news in 1958, with widespread and justified outrage at both the young man and his girlfriend, who maintained that while she watched, she never killed anyone. Starkweather was convicted and executed in 1959. After serving a 17-year prison sentence, Fugate was released.

Turning Starkweather and Kit into relatable characters is an uphill battle, to be sure. Both were clearly psychopaths, and Holly/Caril, their de facto audiences, if not cheerleaders, aren't much more sympathetic. Still, Springsteen evidently saw something of their estrangement from society in himself. As he told Brian Hiatt in a 2010 interview, 'I'm an alienated person by nature. Always have been, still am to this day.'

To musically convey the murderous story of 'Nebraska', Springsteen chose simplicity: fingerpicking three chords on his acoustic guitar. But his voice is so powerful, the guitar barely registers in the overall soundscape. Instead, it's his harmonica that serves to punctuate the song's drama.

As it's printed out on the lyric sheet included with the original album, the story of 'Nebraska' is told in six extended couplets. After the harmonica 'overture', we meet the two characters in the first couplet, then, in the second, get a precis of the action that led to the narrator's conviction: 'From the town of Lincoln, Nebraska, with a sawed-off .410 on my lap/Through to the badlands of Wyoming I killed everything in my path'. The narrator is a distinctly unsympathetic figure, acknowledging to the judge in the third couplet that 'I can't say that I'm sorry for the things that we done/At least for a little while, sir, me and her we had us some fun'.

Things happen quickly in the fourth couplet. Not surprisingly, the narrator is convicted and sentenced to death, then, in the second line, he's suddenly 'in a prison storeroom with leather straps across [his] chest'. In the fifth couplet, a glockenspiel begins to chime, and the narrator speaks to the Sheriff, who is about to pull the switch on the electric chair, telling him that when volts are flowing into his body, to 'make sure my pretty baby is sittin' right there on my lap'.

It's a great last line for a convicted killer, and on first hearing, we might expect the mournful harmonica solo to take us to the end of the song. But, no, the killer has some more last words. Recounting what he has said to people who asked why he went on a senseless killing spree, he gives the supremely lame excuse that 'I guess there's just a meanness in this world'. As the harmonica does, indeed, play its final notes, we're left to reflect on the narrator's last thoughts, which, for better or worse, will haunt the rest of the album.

'Atlantic City' (Springsteen)

If you made a list of all the songs on *Nebraska* that seem like they would be best served when played by a full band, 'Atlantic City' would have to be at the top. It's the closest thing to a rock 'n' roll song on the album. And yet, despite three days spent trying to record it with the E Street Band in April 1982, it didn't come together. Jon Landau recounts in Dave Marsh's *Two Hearts* that

'Atlantic City' 'was one that seemed like it wasn't going to be any problem. And that was going nowhere. No way was it as good as what he had going on that demo tape.'

The song's narrator seems resurrected from *Born To Run*'s 'Meeting Across The River'. This time, though, he is speaking not to his pal Eddie, but to his girlfriend, as he complains about the tough situation he is in. There is no steady work and he has 'debts that no honest man can pay'; therefore, he has decided to 'do a little favor' for a man he met the previous night. Based on the singer's description of Atlantic City – a place that results in mob bosses like the Chicken Man (aka, Philp Charles Testa) getting blown up, where there's 'gonna be a rumble out on the promenade' and 'the gambling commission's hanging on by the skin of its teeth' – it seems more than likely that the 'little favor' he's doing won't turn out well for him.

Acoustic guitar and harmonica are the most noticeable instruments, although Springsteen's Echoplex-drenched backing vocals add another dimension to the music. And the mandolin that comes in during the bridge following the harmonica solo adds an Irish flavor to the song, especially toward the end.

There are some variations, especially in the bridge, but mostly Springsteen plays the same chord pattern – E minor, G, C and G – throughout both the verses and choruses, which gives 'Atlantic City' a feeling of perpetual motion, as though nothing can stop it, or its foolhardy narrator, from moving forward into the deep silence that rises as the song fades to its end.

'Mansion On The Hill' (Springsteen)

Springsteen's maternal grandparents, we learn in his autobiography, lived in a modest farmhouse in New Jersey, but he writes that it 'was a mansion on a hill to me, a citadel of wealth and culture'. Unlike Springsteen, however, the narrator of the song 'Mansion On The Hill' has never been inside the place he gazes upon when his father takes him on evening car rides, an activity which Springsteen tells us in *Born To Run* was one of the few enjoyable things his family did together.

'Mansion On The Hill' is particularly effective at capturing the working-class longing for wealth. The mansion is 'out on the edge of town' – a place that has previously been associated with darkness and despair. But this house rises 'above the factories and the fields'. It is a place where children play behind 'gates of hardened steel', where 'In the summer all the lights would shine/There'd be music playing, people laughing all the time'. Though it's a place he's never been and never will go to, the mansion is central to the narrator's childhood sense of economic inequality. The bottom line, as Springsteen puts it in an earlier song, is 'you can look but you better not touch'.

As he did with Roy Acuff's 'Wreck On The Highway', Springsteen borrowed the title for 'Mansion On The Hill' from another country legend: Hank

Williams. In Williams's song (co-written with Fred Rose), the narrator is singing to a woman who has left him, who lives 'without loving' in order to maintain her wealth, while the singer dwells below, in a cabin in 'the valley'. And yet there are similarities. Like the child and his sister in Springsteen's song, who 'hide out in the tall corn fields' staring up at the place they can never go, Williams's lover gazes up at the light shining 'bright from your window' while 'the trees stand so silent and still'.

Springsteen's song is much quieter than that of Williams and his Drifting Cowboys. The Boss's plaintive harmonica is the solo instrument, with the mandolin, starting at the third verse, softly filling the fourth track of the Tascam 144 recorder. There's nary a minor chord in the song, but 'Mansion On The Hill' is suffused with the hushed melancholy of someone remembering something they wanted but could never have.

'Johnny 99' (Springsteen)

The opening line of 'Johnny 99' references an actual historical occurrence: the 1980 closure of a northern New Jersey Ford assembly plant (at the time, the largest in the country), which had been in operation for 35 years. The song's protagonist, a man named Ralph, who by the end of the verse will be referred to as Johnny 99, ends up with that nickname because, after losing his job at the auto plant and not being able to find other employment, 'He got a gun, shot a night clerk'.

In *Tougher Than The Rest*, June Skinner Sawyers points to two likely precursors to 'Johnny 99' that are found in Folkways' *Anthology Of American Folk Music*, a collection of songs recorded between 1926 and 1933 that evoke what Greil Marcus called 'the old, weird America'. Skinner Sawyers cites Julius Daniels's '99 Year Blues' and the Carter Family's 'John Hardy Was A Desperate Little Man', but, really, Springsteen could have been drawing on any number of folk songs that present us with a reckless person in straitened circumstances.

The songs on the *Anthology Of American Folk Music* often have a dark sense of humor about their characters' problems, and 'Johnny 99' certainly fits that pattern. Granted, the song paints a dismal picture of the protagonist's life. Like 'Nebraska', 'Johnny 99' is about murder and execution. And like the narrator of 'Atlantic City', Ralph/Johnny has 'debts no honest man can pay' – a line so good Springsteen can't refrain from using it twice on the same album.

But tragedy is countered by black comedy, which pairs well with Springsteen's up-tempo strumming on his guitar. The cop who 'slapped the cuffs' on Johnny 99 does so outside what sounds like a punny name for a strip joint, 'the Club Tip Top'. The judge has an over-the-top nickname, 'Mean John Brown', and when he announces Ralph/Johnny's 99-year prison sentence, exaggerated chaos ensues: 'A fist fight broke out in the courtroom, they had to drag Johnny's girl away/His mama stood up and shouted, 'Judge, don't take my boy this way".

Like Gary Gilmore, who in 1977 chose a firing squad over life imprisonment, Johnny 99 prefers death to a life sentence, saying, 'won't you sit back in that chair and think it over, Judge, one more time?' But the request is phrased so casually that it sounds more like he's requesting a beer after closing time than calling for the end of his own life.

That's not to say there isn't a serious side to the song. Springsteen's eerie, drawn-out 'Oh's in the opening signal something bad is in the offing. But the song's energy, in both the singing and guitar and harmonica playing, takes some of the edge off the sorrowful tale of Johnny 99.

'Highway Patrolman' (Springsteen)
A fingerpicked three-chord song, with mandolin and harmonica in the background, 'Highway Patrolman' doesn't break any new musical ground, but it does tell a clear story, with an even clearer thesis: 'A man turns his back on his family, well, he just ain't no good'.

The narrator is Joe Roberts, a highway patrolman in a fictional setting hovering somewhere between Ohio, Michigan and Ontario, Canada. The antagonist is his brother Franky, and, in Joe's own words, 'Franky ain't no good'. Early on, we get a bit of biography about each brother. Joe is a failed wheat farmer who is married to Maria. He joined the highway patrol when farming became untenable. Frank joined the Army from 1965 to 1968 and, presumably, fought in Vietnam. Franky has been trouble 'ever since [the brothers] was young kids', and his return stateside has only made things worse, although Joe continues to cover for him.

The song's crisis comes when Franky nearly kills someone in a roadhouse fight, then flees the scene. Joe gives chase in his cruiser, but when they approach the Canadian border, he stops and – no surprise – lets Franky escape.

Its compelling story aside, 'Highway Patrolman' has probably the most memorable chorus on the album, what Steve Pond called in *Rolling Stone*, 'one of Springsteen's most delicious, delirious reveries': 'Me and Frankie laughin' and drinkin'/Nothing feels better than blood on blood/Takin' turns dancin' with Maria/As the band played 'Night Of The Johnstown Flood''.

Among the several oddities associated with 'Highway Patrolman' is that, prior to its existence, there was no song called 'Night Of The Johnston Flood', although songs with other titles had been written about the catastrophic event in 1889, when more than 2200 Pennsylvanians lost their lives. (And songs *with* that title have been written since.) And then there is Sean Penn's directorial debut, *The Indian Runner*, a mostly forgettable film starring a young Viggo Mortensen that is partly inspired by Springsteen's song, which cannot be blamed for the movie's failings.

'State Trooper' (Springsteen)
Just looking at the title of the last song on side one of *Nebraska*, one might assume that it, like 'Highway Patrolman', was written from the perspective of

a law enforcement officer. But the tag line in this song is 'Mister State Trooper/Please don't stop me'. The singer is running from the law, not failing to enforce it.

'State Trooper' has only two chords, and it sounds like it. There's no harmonica to break the monotony or mandolin to add musical color. Instead, we just have Springsteen's voice, heavily augmented by the Echoplex, begging a state trooper not to stop him.

It's unclear if a state trooper is following the narrator as he drives down the New Jersey turnpike on a rainy night, or whether the singer is simply wishing one would not appear, but despite the fact that this is the most pared-down song on the album, it doesn't feel too long. With Springsteen, to quote Rob Kirkpatrick in *Magic In The Night*, 'fervently strumming his monotonous guitar line', we very much feel that we are there 'in the wee wee hours', while the radio is 'jammed up with talk show stations', inside the thoughts of a man whose mind is nothing short of 'hazy', but whose sense of danger is quite real.

'Used Cars' (Springsteen)

A close cousin of 'Mansion On The Hill', 'Used Cars' is a quiet, fingerpicked song relating a childhood memory of what it's like not to have the things that you want. In the earlier track, the economic disparity focused on property ownership. Here, enlivened by background harmonica and some well-timed taps on the glockenspiel, it's all about automobiles, a subject about which, we know, Springsteen feels passionately.

Like 'Johnny 99', there are some darkly comic touches, although the subject matter isn't nearly as serious. Instead, 'Used Cars' contains some strong autobiographical elements concerning the indignity of not being able to afford a new vehicle.

The details tell us everything. During a test drive of their 'brand new used car', the narrator's little sister is 'in the front seat with an ice cream cone' – these are long before the days of child safety seats, when seatbelts themselves were optional. Meanwhile, his mother is 'in the backseat sittin' all alone'. Back at the auto dealership, his mother 'fingers her wedding band' while the singer tells us that 'the salesman stares at my old man's hands'.

After getting a less-than-stellar deal from the salesman, the family face another humiliation: driving back into the neighborhood with a used, rather than a new, car. As 'the neighbors come from near and far' to gawk, the narrator wishes his father 'would just hit the gas and let out a cry/And tell 'em all they can kiss our asses goodbye'. That doesn't happen, though. The singer's father continues to work 'the same job from mornin' to mornin'', while the narrator walks 'home on the same dirty streets where I was born'.

The chorus, which only appears twice, neatly sums up the feelings of anyone who has ever wanted to buy a new car without being able to. Whether it's winning the lottery or triumphing in some other form of gambling, the sentiment is the same: 'mister the day my number comes in/I ain't ever gonna ride in no used car again'.

'Open All Night' (Springsteen)

The only song on *Nebraska* featuring an electric guitar, 'Open All Night', was, Springsteen wrote in a letter to Landau, a song 'in which the hero braves snow, sleet, rain and the highway patrol for a kiss from his baby's lips'. With a Chuck Berry riff and car-focused lyric that Berry would have been proud to call his own, our echo-saturated singer tells us all about his car – 'I had the carburetor cleaned and checked/With her line blown out she's hummin' like a turbojet' – his gal, Wanda – 'Fried chicken on the front seat, she's sittin' on my lap/We're wipin' our fingers on a Texaco roadmap' – and his travels – 'Gotta hit the gas baby I'm runnin' late/This New Jersey in the mornin' like a lunar landscape'.

Like 'Atlantic City', 'Open All Night' feels as though it would benefit from having the full ensemble join in (check out 2007's *Live In Dublin* for a swinging big band version), but Springsteen is all in on this take, and the song rocks pretty well even as a solo number.

A couple of lines harken directly back to 'State Trooper'. In both songs, we learn that in the 'wee wee hours' your mind gets 'hazy'. As he drives past, the singer notices 'relay towers' along the side of the highway, although in 'State Trooper' he believes they are 'gonna lead me to my baby', while in 'Open All Night' he's not quite so sure: 'Radio relay towers won't you lead me to my baby'. And the radio on 'State Trooper' is 'jammed up with talk show stations', while the programming in 'Open All Night' isn't as obnoxious: 'Radio's jammed up with gospel stations'.

We know that lyrics and music migrate from song to song to song in Springsteen's handwritten drafts and test recordings, but it's interesting to see language so similar in two songs that are only separated by a single album track.

'My Father's House' (Springsteen)

During one of his lengthy spoken introductions in a 1990 concert, Springsteen recounted compulsively driving back in the middle of the night to see his old house in Freehold. When he told his psychiatrist about it, the doctor responded: 'Something went wrong and you keep going back to see if you can fix it.' When Springsteen acknowledged that that was exactly what he was trying to do, the psychiatrist replied: 'Well, you can't.' Nevertheless, he continued, and continues, to try to fix things from his childhood in his songs.

One of Springsteen's many gifts is his ability to make what's important to him feel like it is also important to you, his listener. 'My Father's House' is one of those rare times when the song seems primarily for the benefit of the man who is singing it. Though it's 40 seconds shorter than 'Highway Patrolman', at just over five minutes, 'My Father's House' *feels* like the longest song on the album. No one is interested in your dreams except you, and maybe your psychiatrist, the old saw goes, and the song literally begins: 'Last night I dreamed that I was a child'.

Part of what makes 'My Father's House' so tortuous is that the narrator spends half the song recounting just getting to his father's dream house: through a forest 'out where the pines grow wild and tall', past fields from which 'ghostly voices' arise, with 'branches and brambles' scratching at his arms even as he arrives and falls 'shaking' into his father's arms.

There's a harmonica break, then the singer tells us he awoke, wished things had been different and then decided to drive to the actual house of his childhood memories. In the fourth verse, he oddly addresses someone as 'sir' – even taking into account how much 'sir' and 'mister' are tics of Springsteen's writing, that feels weird. And it's even weirder that the narrator is expecting his father to be living in their family house when he should know perfectly well that is not the case. A woman tells him 'through a chained door', 'I'm sorry, son, but no one by that name lives here anymore'. Well, duh.

The sixth and final verse – there is no chorus – attempts to bring the dream and real life together: 'My father's house shines hard and bright/It stands like a beacon calling me in the night'. That works fairly well, but then Springsteen strains too hard for meaning at the end, when we learn that the house 'shining 'cross this dark highway' is 'Where our sins lie unatoned'. What sins? Whose sins? Why are they unatoned?

Sometimes, it's better to keep our dreams to ourselves.

'Reason To Believe' (Springsteen)

Nebraska ends with a classic Springsteen paradox: a song with a bouncy major chord vibe and an optimistic title, 'Reason To Believe', that is entirely depressing in the verse lyrics.

In the first verse, we meet a man poking a dead dog with a stick. He's 'kinda puzzled' by death, apparently believing that 'if he stood there long enough/That dog'd get up and run'. In verse two, Mary Lou is the sap. She loves Johnny so much that she brings her pay home to him every day. However, Johnny – Springsteen isn't going to win any awards for the most original character names – dumps Mary Lou, leaving her waiting 'down at the end of that dirt road/For young Johnny to come back'.

There's a moment of positivity, as a baby named Kyle William is baptized in the river. But in the second half of the verse, Kyle's new life is juxtaposed with that of an old man dying in 'a whitewashed shotgun shack'. They do take the old man's body to the graveyard to pray for him, and in the final full verse, we are again treated to a scene of celebration. A young man is about to be married, and the congregation is gathered around the riverside as the 'Groom stands waiting for his bride'. But it's too much to hope for a happy ending in this song, and after a while everyone departs, leaving the groom 'Wondering where can his baby be'.

Even the chorus pokes fun at people's unfounded hopefulness: 'Struck me kind of funny/Seemed kind of funny, sir, to me'. Are we all just idiots, pressing on despite knowing that everything will *not* come out all right in the end? Possibly. Does that bother the Boss? Maybe, but that doesn't keep him from calling it as he sees it. In any case, the chorus keeps insisting, 'at the end of every hard-earned day/People find some reason to believe'. True that.

Bonus Track
'The Big Payback' (Springsteen)
B-side of 'Open All Night'
A little rockabilly ditty of less than two minutes, 'The Big Payback' employs three familiar chords to tell a familiar story. A working man keeps 'a sweatin' like all get out'. He works so long that he's 'a losin' track/Waitin', waitin' on the big payback'. In the final verse, fed up, he finally quits his job and gets 'a knife … long and black', planning to head down to the alley for the big payback, apparently from the boss who's been mistreating him.

All the music is made with Springsteen's harmonica, electric guitar and his voice. The latter two are saturated in echo, and this *Nebraska*-era outtake sounds like it could be an outtake from Johnny Burnett, circa 1957. Like the A-side of the single, 'Open All Night', 'The Big Payback' is an up-tempo number that's worth a listen, but it does feel more like a novelty track than something worthy of inclusion on *The Essential Bruce Springsteen*, the title of the 2003 CD on which it later appeared, albeit on the 'bonus disc'.

Born In The U.S.A. (1984)

Personnel:
Bruce Springsteen: lead vocals, guitar
Roy Bittan: synthesizer, piano, backing vocals
Clarence Clemons: saxophone, percussion, backing vocals
Danny Federici: Hammond organ, glockenspiel, piano ('Born In The U.S.A.')
Garry Tallent: bass guitar, backing vocals
Steven Van Zandt: acoustic guitar, mandolin, harmony vocals
Max Weinberg: drums, backing vocals
Richie 'La Bamba' Rosenberg: backing vocals ('Cover Me' and 'No Surrender')
Ruth Jackson: backing vocals ('My Hometown')
Recorded at Power Station and Hit Factory, New York City, between January 1982 and March 1984
Producers: Bruce Springsteen, Jon Landau, Chuck Plotkin, Steven Van Zandt
Release date: 4 June 1984
Running time: 46:41
Label: Columbia
Album charts: US: 1, UK: 1
Singles charts: 'Dancing In The Dark' (US: 2, UK: 4); 'Cover Me' (US: 7, UK: 16); 'Born In The U.S.A.' (US: 9; UK: 11); 'I'm On Fire' (US: 6, UK: 20); 'Glory Days' (US: 5, UK: 17); 'I'm Goin' Down' (US: 9); 'My Hometown' (US: 6, UK: 9)

Born In The U.S.A. is Springsteen's most popular album, if not his most beloved. When the album debuted at number nine on the *Billboard* Charts and then moved to number one a few weeks later, it seemed destined to be a smash hit, but its origins are somewhat more complicated. Indeed, in *Songs*, Springsteen says that aside from the title track, 'The rest of the album contains a group of songs about which I've always had some ambivalence.'

Many of the 12 songs on *Born In The U.S.A.* existed in some incarnation when Springsteen was recording *Nebraska*. There is, for instance, a very punk version of 'Born In The U.S.A.' on *Nebraska '82*, the box set released in 2025. And you can listen to songs recorded between the two albums that didn't make the *Born In The U.S.A.* cut on both *Tracks* (1998) and the *LA Garage Sessions '83* disc on *Tracks II* (2025). What we hear is Springsteen trying to figure out how to feature the stripped-down country-folk he was drawn to while still embracing the rock 'n' roll that made him famous. At one point, he even considered releasing a double-album, with the acoustic *Nebraska* on one LP, and the electric *Born In The U.S.A.* on the other. Fortunately, he realized how jarring that would be for listeners and kept the two records separate.

Still, at the very end of 'Reason To Believe', the final song on *Nebraska*, there is the faintest hint of a synthesizer, which seems to foreshadow how full that instrument, along with Max Weinberg's crashing drums, would come to dominate some of the songs on *Born In The U.S.A.* It was that big rock 'n' roll *sound*, as much as Springsteen's singing and lyrics, that took America, and then the world, by storm in the second half of 1984 and the first half of 1985. Granted, many of the songs on *Born In The U.S.A.* employ the time-honored combination of Roy Bittan on piano and Danny Federici on organ, but it's impossible to ignore Bittan's brand-new Yamaha CS-80 synthesizer on songs like the title track, 'Downbound Train' and 'Dancing In The Dark'. His keyboard fills those songs with shimmering swells and electronic sheen. Admittedly, the synthesizers featured on *Born In The U.S.A.* and, later, *Tunnel Of Love* sound dated now to some ears, but in the mid- and late 1980s, they were very much au courant.

The first CD ever mass manufactured in the United States, *Born In The U.S.A.* was, Springsteen writes in his autobiography, 'the biggest album of my career', giving him an incredible run of seven top ten singles from one album – at the time tying the record held by Michael Jackson for *Thriller*. (It would be decades before Katy Perry would break that record with eight top ten singles, from her 2010 album *Teenage Dream*.) Springsteen had a right to be proud: 'Along with Madonna, Prince, Michael Jackson and the stars of disco, I was a bona fide mainstream radio 'superstar'... *Born In The U.S.A.* changed my life, gave me my largest audience, forced me to think harder about the way I presented my music and set me briefly at the center of the pop world.'

It was quite a climb for the kid from blue-collar Freehold, New Jersey, who'd been inspired by watching Elvis Presley and The Beatles on the *Ed Sullivan Show*. Now, here he was, maybe not quite as big as his heroes, but definitely getting there.

The iconic cover of *Born In The U.S.A.*, taken by famed photographer Annie Leibovitz, looks very patriotic. In the background are the red and white stripes of an American flag. In the foreground is the Boss – and his butt. His tan and not-so-skinny arms are cut off at the top of the frame, but we can tell they are extending from a white T-shirt. The left arm is held at his side, while his right hand is shoved into the pocket of his worn and faded blue jeans, which are held up by a snazzy leather belt. In the right-hand pocket is a washed-out red baseball cap, belonging to the recently deceased father of a friend. Nowadays, we would associate a red cap with Donald Trump and his MAGA movement, but, of course, back then, it was just there to complete the color scheme. The title and the artist's name are in blue all caps at the very top, but mostly what we have is a photograph, one so good, in fact, that it's also the flip side of the cover.

Rolling Stone was predictably enthusiastic about the album. Debby Miller wrote, 'Though the characters are dying of longing for some sort of payoff from the American dream, Springsteen's exuberant voice and the swell of the music inform you that they haven't given up.' She adds: 'A great dancer himself, Springsteen puts an infectious beat under his songs.'

Writing in the *New York Times*, Stephen Holden saw the continuity of the new album with the Boss's earlier work: 'If *Born In The U.S.A.* is an elegy to a vanishing breed of American, Bruce Springsteen represents a spirit that is also disappearing from our popular music. He is one of a very small number of rock performers who use rock to express an ongoing epic vision of this country, individual social roots and the possibility of heroic self-creation.'

Even grumpy Robert Christgau chose *Born In The U.S.A.* as the best album of 1984 for the *Village Voice*'s annual Pazz & Jop Poll, giving it an 'A+' in his *Consumer Guide*. Arguing that Springsteen's 'apparent retrenchment' from folk to rock 'n' roll, in fact, signaled that he 'has evolved', Christgau called *Born In The U.S.A.* Springsteen's 'most rhythmically propulsive, vocally incisive, lyrically balanced and commercially undeniable album.'

'Born In The U.S.A.' (Springsteen)

Like 'Born To Run', 'Born In The U.S.A.' is the center of its album's orbit. However, rather than opening side two like its predecessor, 'Born In The U.S.A.' comes at us right out of the gate, both guns blasting. In *Songs*, Springsteen describes the sound of the track as 'martial, modal and straight ahead', and that's what we get: Max Weinberg's snare drum like a repeated slap across the face, and Roy Bittan's synthesizer driving home the unforgettable six-note hook. Federci plays a piano chord in the empty space after the riff, but that's the only note of subtlety in this two-chord song, especially once Springsteen sing-yells the opening lines: 'Born down in a dead man's town/The first kick I took was when I hit the ground'.

Inspired by Vietnam veteran Ron Kovic's memoir *Born On The 4th Of July*, 'Born In The U.S.A.' tells the story of an unnamed man sent off to Vietnam after getting 'in a little hometown jam'. After he returns home from killing 'the yellow man' – a phrase Springsteen would surely not use if the song were written today – the singer fails to find work at his hometown refinery and does not receive the necessary care from the Veterans' administration.

In the fourth verse, we learn that the narrator had a brother who died in the Battle at Khe Sanh in 1968, and that they still have a picture of a Vietnamese woman the brother was in love with. In the fifth verse, which is not separated by the booming, ironic chorus of 'Born in the U.S.A./I was born in the U.S.A.', we get a final picture of the singer's bleak life. 'Down in the shadow of the penitentiary/Out by the gas fires of the refinery', he has been 'ten years burning down the road', but he still has 'Nowhere to run, ain't got nowhere to go'.

'Born In The U.S.A.' is quite obviously an *anti*-war song, and yet the album was released in June of a US presidential election, and – with its red, white and blue cover, and, when taken completely out of context, the song's apparently patriotic chorus – 'Born In The U.S.A.' quickly became fodder for right-wing media and politicians. In September 1984, *Washington Post* columnist George Will turned Springsteen's vaunted work ethic and working-class background upside down:

In an age of lackadaisical effort and slipshod products, anyone who does anything – anything legal – conspicuously well and with zest is a national asset. Springsteen's tour is hard, honest work and evidence of the astonishing vitality of America's regions and generations. They produce distinctive tones of voice that other regions and generations embrace. There is still nothing quite like being born in the U.S.A.

Not long afterwards, making a campaign stop in Hammonton, New Jersey, Ronald Reagan himself added to the hooey: 'America's future rests in a thousand dreams inside your hearts. It rests in the message of hope in the songs of a man so many young Americans admire: New Jersey's own, Bruce Springsteen.'

In an interesting twist, being embraced by the right forced Springsteen to become clearer about his own left-leaning politics. As Gillian Gaar points out in 'Bruce Springsteen's Political Journey from 'Born In The U.S.A.' to '41 Shots'', when *Born In The U.S.A.* was released, Springsteen 'was hardly the outspoken activist and advocate that he is today … Previously, he been the kind of artist who let his songs do the talking. But now he had to specify exactly where he stood, if for no other reason than to prevent his message from being hijacked.'

The result was that, in years to come, he would be a reliable campaigner for Democratic presidential candidates from John Kerry and Barack Obama, with whom he would co-author the book *Renegades: Born In The USA*, to Hilary Clinton, Joe Biden and Kamala Harris.

'Cover Me' (Springsteen)

At the request of David Geffen, Springsteen wrote a version of this song, entitled 'Drop On Down And Cover Me' for Donna Summer: 'She could really sing,' he explains in *Songs*, 'and I disliked the veiled racism of the anti-disco movement.'

With Springsteen's straight-ahead rock 'n' roll beat, nasty lead guitar and snarling vocals, it's hard to imagine 'Cover Me' as a disco song, but it's not hard to see why it became one of his biggest singles. There's an urgency not only to the riff, but to the band's playing, and the background vocals, provided by Richie Rosenberg, who, many years later, would play trombone with Max Weinberg and The Tonight Show Band, absolutely soar.

For a Springsteen song, the lyrics are fairly generic, with lots of repetition on the theme of the singer asking his baby to cover him from anything bad, including 'the rain, the driving snow' and 'the wild wind blowing'. Then again, that economy of expression may well be another reason for the song's success on the radio during the late summer of 1984: it went to number seven in the US and number 16 in the UK.

It's notable that a demo for the song recorded at the Hit Factory in 1982 included what Margotin and Guesdon call in *All The Songs*, 'one of the best guitar solos the Boss ever played.' However, when it came time to rerecord 'Cover Me' two years later at The Power Station, Springsteen was unable to recapture the magic of his solo, so it's that earlier instrumental track we have on *Born In The U.S.A.*

'Darlington County' (Springsteen)

The origin of 'Darlington County' goes way back to the fecund late 1970s writing sessions for *Darkness On The Edge Of Town*, though it feels more like a song that would be at home on *The River*. 'Darlington County' is a raucous country-rock tune, with a hillbilly introduction from Springsteen and heavy on the guitars throughout. Weinberg hits his amplified snare like he's angry and just can't pound its skin hard enough, while Federici's organ plays the hook atop Bittan's piano.

The lyrics are in the classic Springsteen comic mode, with more than a touch of *carpe diem* in his appeal to the current apple of his eye. Our two protagonists are the narrator and his cousin Wayne, who have driven 800 miles down from New York to South Carolina 'without seeing a cop', with 'rock and roll music blastin' off the T-Top' of their muscle car. They feel like their luck has only gotten better when they meet up with a 'little girl, standing on the corner', and try to convince her to ride off with them because they are so wealthy that their 'Pas each own one of the World Trade Centers', a wisecracking line that would be forever touched with sorrow 17 years in the future.

The country feel is given a bit of soul with Clemons's sax solo after the second chorus, which is simply 'Sha la la la', etc. In the final verse, we learn the singer hasn't seen his cousin in a week; he is told by the 'County man' that if Wayne 'don't work … he don't get paid'.

Evidently, the connection between the cousins was not a close one because the narrator is soon ready to make a quick exit, presumably with the 'little girl' from verse two at his side. On the way out, he sees 'Wayne handcuffed to the bumper of a state trooper's Ford'. But there's no time to stop when you're having this much fun, and off he drives, singing 'Sha la la, sha la la la la', all the way out of Darlington County on the way to his next adventure.

'Working On The Highway' (Springsteen)

The peppiest song on *Born In The U.S.A.* is also the one with the most dubious premise. Originally a slow, fingerpicked number called 'Child Bride' that was intended for *Nebraska*, 'Working On The Highway' has basically the same lyrics as the earlier song but an entirely different feel and beat. It's about a man arrested and put on a highway chain gang for having underage sex with a 'little girl'. What's strange is that, other than his arrest, for unnamed reasons, it would be hard to identify the fact that he had committed a crime because Springsteen refers to 'little girls' so often throughout his oeuvre. Indeed, there's a little girl in the preceding song, 'Darlington County' and there's another one coming up two songs later in 'I'm On Fire'. Most Springsteen fans think of 'little girl' as simply a term of endearment for someone slightly younger than the singer, but 'Working On The Highway' throws something of a monkey wrench into those interpretations.

The song begins deceptively. The first two verses of this rockabilly number, which is musically close kin to 'Darlington County', present us with another of Springsteen's hardworking characters. It's Friday night, and this particular gentleman is, like so many Springsteen protagonists before him, reflecting on what people are going to do after work: 'Some heading home to their families, some looking to get hurt/Some going down to Stovall wearing trouble on their shirts'. In the second verse, the singer seems to have different plans. Vowing, 'Someday, mister, I'm gonna lead a better life than this', he tells us that in his 'head [he] keeps a picture of a pretty little miss'.

So far, there are no real red flags – other than the one the narrator holds while watching 'the traffic pass [him] by' – and the chorus simply tells us about his work on the highway, 'laying down the blacktop' and 'blasting through the bedrock'. The third verse describes his meeting with his pretty little miss: 'One day I looked straight at her and she looked straight back'. Again, it sounds like just another love story, and even in the bridge, when her father says, 'Son, can't you see that she's just a little girl?/She don't know nothing about this cruel, cruel world', we can't help but recall how deadset Rosalita's father was against the narrator back on *The Wild, The Innocent & The E Street Shuffle*.

It's only when the singer tells us that after they fled to Florida, her brothers came and got her, and he was arrested, that we learn he has committed an actual crime. Here, knowing the song was previously called 'Child Bride' allows us to put all the pieces together and understand why 'the judge got mad and put [him] straight away'. The 'work bell clang' the narrator hears every morning is sounding in prison: he is not a *voluntary* member of the Charlotte County road gang.

But there's no time for reflecting on the consequences of his actions. The catchy chorus is back. There's been lots of handclapping along the way, and Weinberg's drums and Tallent's bass create an irresistible rhythm. Nevertheless, 'Working On The Highway' puts up a roadblock, as it were, for listeners who would prefer to imagine that the seduction of young women across Springsteen's catalog of songs is always hunky dory, and, indeed, legal.

'Downbound Train' (Springsteen)

In *The Stories Behind The Songs*, Brian Hiatt quotes Bittan on his efforts to convince Springsteen and the other members of the band of the value of his new Yamaha synthesizer. 'We started those sessions, and I brought the synthesizer in, and you would have thought I'd killed somebody.' And yet, ultimately, Springsteen realized that with a synthesizer, 'you could change the landscape. You could broaden it ... It could be something anonymous and evoke something entirely different.' In fact, it would become an instrument that the Boss very much made his own on his next studio album.

On 'Downbound Train', the synthesizer is used to emphasize the moody and melancholy life of the narrator, a man who lost his job at the lumber yard just before his 'love went bad, times got hard'. But we don't hear the instrument right away. Initially, the song sounds like it will be another mid-tempo guitar, bass and drum rocker, with the first verse ending with an unintentionally comic image: 'I work down at the car wash/Where all it ever does is rain'.

In the second verse, the synthesizer comes on board, lightly at first, as the narrator's woman leaves him. Like some character from a 1940s country song, she hops on board a train, which allows him, in his dreams, to 'hear that whistle whining' and 'feel her kiss in the misty rain'.

The synthesizer plays the solo, then all the musicians except Bittan drop out, as Springsteen relates a dream very much like the one at the beginning of 'My Father's House' on *Nebraska*. In excessive detail, he describes running through the woods in the moonlight to the couple's 'wedding house'. But, of course, there's no one there, and in the final lines we learn, in a fast-forward, that the narrator has joined a 'railroad gang' (not dissimilar to the 'road gang' of the previous song) so that he can work in the rain and hear the train's lonesome whistle, which painfully, but somehow necessarily, reminds him of the love he has lost.

'I'm On Fire' (Springsteen)
The shortest song on *Born In The U.S.A.*, and the last song on side one, 'I'm On Fire' was also the album's fourth single, reaching number six in the US and number five in the UK.

It's a pared-down sound compared to shouters like 'Born In The U.S.A.' and 'Cover Me'. In one speaker, we hear Springsteen fast-picking his electric guitar. In the other speaker, Weinberg plays a steady but muted drum beat. In the center are Bittan's quiet synthesizer and Springsteen's moody vocals. For a love song, it has a distinctly downbeat feel, though, as he has so often in the past, the Boss manages to build a memorable melody around just four chords.

After 'Working On The Highway', we might feel a bit uncomfortable about the singer's open gambit to win the hand of the person he is addressing: 'Hey, little girl, is your daddy home?/Did he go away and leave you all alone?' We don't *want* to think the narrator is a pervert, that the object of his desire truly is a little girl and that the man who left her 'all alone' is her literal father, rather than an older boyfriend. Surely that can't be correct, yet the earlier song troubles the waters.

In any event, after the brief, cliché second verse and the slight chorus – 'Oh, oh, oh/I'm on fire' – Bittan plays a few notes on the synthesizer to serve as a solo, and there's an abrupt change in the quality of the lyrics. Now, we learn the full depth of the singer's desire: 'it's like someone took a knife, baby, edgy and dull/And cut a six-inch valley through the middle of my skull/At night, I wake up with the sheets soakin' wet/And a freight train runnin' through the middle of my head'. Whoever he is singing to, it's no ordinary passion he's feeling as the synthesizer whispers of desire and the singer shouts out his wordless and echoing pain while the song fades to its close.

'No Surrender' (Springsteen)

Side two begins with all the band members, save Clarence, rocking their instruments in an introduction that once again features the majestic background vocals of Richie 'La Bamba' Rosenberg. Then, 25 seconds in, Springsteen offers up one of his best lyrics: concise without being cryptic, fully fleshed out without being verbose.

The story is of two friends, who 'swore blood brothers against the wind' as teenagers, and have managed to retain the friendship into adulthood. The first two verses are nostalgic, containing memorable lines like 'We learned more from a three-minute record, baby/Than we ever learned in school' and 'I hear your sister's voice calling us home/Across the open yards/Well, maybe we'll cut someplace of our own/With these drums and these guitars'.

The final verse moves to the present, with the singer's friend telling him, 'There's a war outside still raging', and claiming, 'it ain't ours anymore to win'. But the narrator rejects that pessimistic outlook, and instead dreams of sleeping with his lover, 'With a wide-open country in my eyes/And these romantic dreams in my head'. That assertion of optimism fits well with the chorus and the 'promise' the two friends swore they would 'always remember'.

The music is three chords of unstoppable rock, never changing tempo throughout the song's four minutes. There's no solo to interrupt the flow, just the chord progression of the last line of the chorus with 'Lay lay lay lay lay lay lay' replacing the tag.

In *Songs*, Springsteen says that he didn't intend to include the song on *Born In The U.S.A.* He was uncomfortable with the lyrics because 'You don't hold out and triumph all the time in life. You compromise, you suffer defeat; you slip into life's gray areas.' In short, real life is the opposite of the chorus's victorious message: 'No defeat, baby, no surrender'. And yet, Steve Van Zandt, the friend who was the inspiration for the song, was adamant that 'No Surrender' belonged on the album, arguing that 'the portrait of friendship and the song's expression of the inspirational power of rock music was an important part of the picture.'

Van Zandt was already pursuing solo projects with his new band, Little Steven and the Disciples of Soul, and though he hadn't yet officially quit the E Street Band – he would do that before they began touring in support of the album – he does not play guitar on this song. He was clearly moving in a different direction than Springsteen. Still, 'No Surrender', and the song that followed, showed the Boss pledging his loyalty to old friends.

'Bobby Jean' (Springsteen)

Is 'Bobby Jean' also about Steven Van Zandt? In *Songs*, Springsteen simply refers to 'Bobby Jean' as 'a good song about youthful friendship', but in a

1984 interview, Don McLeese asks the Boss straight out: 'Is [Van Zandt] Bobby Jean?' Springsteen's reply is cagey: 'That's just a song about friendship. I'm sure I drew on missing him, but it's not real specific about it.' Still, while playing this song in concert, Springsteen sometimes has images of Van Zandt projected on the screens around the venue, so it's pretty clear that Bobby Jean, with her/his/their deliberately non-gender-specific name, is at least partially a stand-in for Van Zandt. While Van Zandt plays rhythm guitar on the majority of tracks on *Born In The U.S.A.*, as is the case with 'No Surrender', he is absent here.

The song begins with the narrator visiting the home of his old friend Bobby Jean, only to learn from their mother that Bobby Jean has gone away to someplace unnamed. Immediately, the singer feels loss and nostalgia for their friendship, which began when they were both 16: 'We liked the same music/ We liked the same bands/We liked the same clothes'. The narrator knows he will miss Bobby Jean, but he cherishes the memories of the times they spent together, and he sends his song out to Bobby Jean on the radio to let them know he is thinking of them.

The song's chord progression evokes the mixed feelings of the lyrics. There's a major chord, followed by a minor chord, followed by another major chord, then the pattern ends with a major seventh. A feeling of warmth and good-heartedness is provided by the major chords, the minor chord evokes a touch of sadness and the major seventh adds a note of bittersweet nostalgia.

The band capture all of those emotions, with Bittan playing both synthesizer and piano, and Federici conjuring memories of songs from past years with the glockenspiel. The rhythm section of Tallent and Weinberg keeps steady time on a track that, with all the keyboards, occasionally feels like it wants to head in the direction of schmaltz. Fortunately, Clemons's long solo at the end puts everything to rights.

In the second verse, the singer says to Bobby Jean: 'Now I wished you would have told me/I wished I could have talked to you/Just to say, 'Goodbye, Bobby Jean''. Interestingly, we learn from a chapter in Springsteen's autobiography entitled 'Buona Fortuna, Fratello Mio' (Good Luck, My Brother) that the two men *did* actually sit down and talk out Van Zandt's reasons for leaving: he wanted to 'move to the center mic' and lead his own group. It sounds like a fraught conversation, but we know that in the years to come, after his star turn as Silvio Dante on *The Sopranos*, Van Zandt would return to the fold as a valued and full-time member of the E Street Band. There was a second act for Bobby Jean.

'I'm Goin' Down' (Springsteen)

How, one wonders, does he do it? 'I'm Goin' Down' uses the same four chords for both verse and chorus. Although there are some changes in the dynamics, especially after the brief sax solo from Clemons, the tempo pretty much stays the same for the entire three and a half minutes.

And yet 'I'm Goin' Down' is as catchy as they come in the Springsteen catalog. Partly that has to do with the fine guitar work by Springsteen and Van Zandt, and Federci's Hammond B-3 sailing above Bittan's piano, not to mention the smack of Weinberg's drums, which mixer Bob Clearmountain once again brings to the forefront. Partly it's due to the easy-to-remember and easy-to-croon chorus lyric, which is simply the title sung four times, with three 'down's added at the end of each line.

The story told in the verse is also one that plenty of listeners can relate to: a love affair that's gradually gone cold for one of the parties – in this case, the woman the singer is addressing. Instead of the passion that once kept them together, he elicits from her only 'bored sighs' and, according to the narrator, lately she 'gets [her] kicks from just driving [him] down, down, down, down'.

Recorded at the Power Station in 1982, 'I'm Goin' Down' was the sixth single from *Born In The U.S.A.*, peaking at number nine in the US, although failing to chart in the UK. As Springsteen fiddled with the final track list for the album, the song almost lost out to 'Pink Cadillac', which would have been a shame. With its good-time comic energy, 'Pink Cadillac' would have spoiled the delicate balance between striving and regret on side two.

'Glory Days' (Springsteen)

At its best, Springsteen's music is timeless. On balance, his music videos are not. The video for 'Glory Days' is pure mid-1980s. *Yikes*! It opens with Springsteen at the wheel of a piece of heavy machinery, then cuts to him throwing baseballs at a square of wood. Soon, we are in a small, crowded club, Maxwell's in Hoboken, with the Boss and the E Street Band lip-synching and mugging for the cameras. It's a mixed-up crew, including Nils Lofgren and Patty Scialfa, who were in the new touring band, but not on the recording, and Steven Van Zandt, playing guitar and singing harmony vocals, as he does on the recording – although he had already left the band when the video was shot. The video ends with Springsteen pitching again, this time to his son, until his wife, played presciently by Sicalfa, tells them it's time to come on home.

In the song's first verse, the singer runs into an old friend who 'was a big baseball player/Back in high school'. In the second verse, he meets up with a female friend who, 'Back in school … could turn all the boys' heads'. Both of them seem to have left their best years in the past and are now running on the fumes of 'glory days', which pass us by 'in the wink of a young girl's eye'. In the final verse, the singer comments that he, too, will probably someday sit around 'trying to recapture/A little of the glory' of days gone by. In his note on the song in the *Greatest Hits* booklet (1995), Springsteen says: 'The first verse actually happened, the second verse mostly happened, the third verse is happening now.'

The feel of 'Glory Days' is fun and party-like, which is admittedly captured by the cheesy mimed performance in the video. Tallent's pulsing bass and

Weinberg's crashing snares keep the song moving forward, with Federici's organ playing the hook in the intro and outro as well as during and after each chorus. The back-and-forth vocals between Springsteen and Van Zandt in the song's final minute keep the energy from flagging.

Still, for all its tongue-in-cheek observations on glory days, there's a hint of pity in the descriptions of people whose best days were in high school and who must live out the long decades afterwards as has-beens and might-have-beens.

'Dancing In The Dark' (Springsteen)
For those who were around during the early glory days of MTV, 'Dancing In The Dark' – Springsteen's highest-charting US single ever, at number two – seemed omnipresent. The video, which featured a newly-muscled Springsteen pulling a young Courtney Cox from the audience to dance with him on stage, was everywhere.

Toward the end of the recording sessions for *Born In The U.S.A.*, Jon Landau, so the story goes, didn't hear a hit, and he asked Springsteen to go home and write one, just as, way back in 1972, Clive Davis had instructed the Boss to bring in something more commercial for *Asbury Park*. Miraculously, just as he had penned 'Blinded By The Light' and 'Spirit In The Night' in a few days, 'Dancing In The Dark' suddenly appeared. In *Born To Run*, Springsteen calls his big hit 'My song about my own alienation, fatigue and desire to get out from inside the studio, my room, my record, my head.'

With lyrics like 'Man, I'm just tired and bored with myself' and 'They say you gotta stay hungry/Hey, baby, I'm just about starving tonight', the words of 'Dancing In The Dark' certainly signal the alienation and fatigue Springsteen was feeling. But the music, even with its prominent minor chords, is driving and dance-oriented (a club remix by Arthur Baker made it the best-selling 12" single of 1984). Then there's Bittan's synthesizer riff – a little melancholy, yes, but played so fast that most of the sorrow is squeezed out of the music, even when factoring in Clemons's late-night solo in the outro.

And, of course, for those who have seen the video, there is always the image of Springsteen smiling and dancing his way through the song, as though it were actually about a different topic altogether, a song that might be better suited with a title like 'Dancing In The Light'.

'My Hometown' (Springsteen)
'My Hometown' was the seventh top ten US single from the album, though it's hard to imagine this brooding meditation on a dying town making the charts if it hadn't been for the six previous hits.

Like the boy in *Nebraska*'s 'Mansion On The Hill', and like Springsteen himself, the child in the first stanza spends memorable time with his father simply driving around their town. Indeed, the father is so keen to have the son experience what it's like to travel the streets of his hometown that he sets the child 'on his lap in that big old Buick' and allows him to pretend as though he is steering the car. We know from his autobiography how fraught Springsteen's relationship was with his father, but this memory, despite the 1950s-era disregard for child safety, is a fond one, with the father even tousling his son's hair.

The second verse rockets us forward to 1965, when 'tension was running high' "tween the black and white' at the narrator's high school. The shotgun blast between two cars stopped at a light did, according to Springsteen's autobiography, actually take place during those 'troubled times' in Freehold.

In the bridge, we get a current picture of the singer's hometown, and it isn't a pretty one. Main Street is deserted, with nothing but 'whitewashed windows and vacant stores'. In addition, 'They're closing down the textile mill across the railroad tracks', and the foreman is forthright with those who will be losing their employment: 'These jobs are going, boys/And they ain't coming back/To your hometown'.

In the final verse, the narrator tells us that he and his wife have been 'Talking about getting out/Packing up our bags, maybe heading south'. The singer is 35 and has a son of his own, whom he also dubiously decides to prop up 'behind the wheel' of his car while they drive around, and the narrator repeats what his father said to him: 'This is your hometown'.

During the first verse and chorus, Bittan's synthesizer is the main instrument, with Weinberg's bass drum and Clemons's tambourine keeping time. Things pick up with the second verse, with Springsteen's guitar, Tallent's bass and Federici's organ joining in, but the music remains subservient to the singing, with the stark chorus simply being variations on phrases about the speaker's hometown. In the final minute, the backing vocals of Ruth Jackson become more prominent, as Bittan plays the riff and the song very slowly fades to silence.

Bonus Tracks
'Pink Cadillac' (Springsteen)
B-side of 'Dancing In The Dark'
'Pink Cadillac' was originally recorded as an acoustic version during the *Nebraska* sessions in 1982. In 1984, Springsteen recorded a full band version, with the intention of putting the song on *Born In The U.S.A*. It didn't make the final cut, but its release as the B-side of 'Dancing In The Dark', Springsteen's biggest hit, didn't hurt. While 'Pink Cadillac' didn't officially chart on *Billboard*'s Top 100, it did reach number 27 on the *Top Tracks* listing, which ranks the most-played songs on rock radio.

'Pink Cadillac' is mostly comic, with the speaker telling the object of his affection that he doesn't love her for her money, he's already 'got plenty of that'. Instead, and even though she gets on his nerves, he loves her for her pink Cadillac, with its 'crushed velvet seats'. He imagines having 'a party' with her in the backseat, and wonders what she may do with other men in that inviting locale when he's not with her.

The song contains some wonderful hyperbole: 'They say Eve tempted Adam with an apple/Man, I ain't going for that/I know it was her pink Cadillac' and 'My love is bigger than a Honda/It's bigger than a Subaru'; therefore, there is 'only one thing/And one car that will do'.

The music, too, is fun. Often compared to the *Peter Gunn* theme, *sans* keyboards, the riff, built on a three-chord blues, chugs along effortlessly on Springsteen's guitar, just like a … well, you know.

In a 2006 interview with Phil Sutcliffe for *Mojo* magazine, Springsteen offered a thoughtful response to the working-class fascination with fancy cars and material wealth: 'I'm a child of Woody and Elvis. They may not be opposite ends of the spectrum. Elvis was an instrument of revolutionary change. Elvis drove a pink Cadillac and Woody wrote a song about a Cadillac. He was not dismissive of those pleasures … You live with the contradictions.'

Bette Midler recorded 'Pink Cadillac' for a 1983 album, but Springsteen blocked its release, arguing that the song wasn't meant to be sung by a woman. It's ironic, therefore, that in 1988 Natalie Cole was permitted to release a version that cracked the *Billboard* top ten.

'Shut Out The Light' (Springsteen)

B-side of 'Born In The U.S.A.'

For all the nitwits who couldn't figure out that 'Born In The U.S.A.' was an anti-war song, there is its B-side, 'Shut Out The Light', about a returning Vietnam veteran suffering from what we would now call Post-Traumatic Stress Disorder.

'Shut Out The Light' is a well-told story about a man named Johnson Laneer coming back from the war. In the first verse, he watches from the plane window as 'the runway rushed up at him as he felt the wheels touch down'. He heads for a bar downtown where he meets his wife, who loosens 'an extra button on her blouse' before going to meet her husband.

However, things aren't good for Johnson. His family doesn't seem to understand him, and the most comfort his father can offer is that he is 'sure they'd give him his job back down at the factory'. In the final verse, Johnson is in a 'dark forest … filled with rain', standing in the 'cold back water' of a river and looking out at the city lights.

Springsteen taps the tambourine for rhythm, and plays a bit of harmonica, but mostly the music comes from his two acoustic guitars: one picked, one strummed. The other notable instrument is a bluegrass violin played by Soozie Tyrell, who would later tour extensively with the E Street Band. She adds a poignant touch to the lyrics, beginning with the second verse.

The B-side version is a half-minute shorter than the version on the disc for *LA Garage Sessions '83* on 2025's *Tracks II*. That's because it restores two missing verses, which paint a much darker picture of Johnson Laneer's situation. The missing verse before the second chorus suggests that the reason Johnson has the shakes and lies awake until the morning is because he's addicted to heroin: 'Just him and a few bad habits he'd brought back from there'. And in the final verse of the full song, he's not just standing in the water, but he's waiting for it to end his life: 'Now he watches the water of that nameless river rise above his chest'.

Was this earlier version too grim a picture for the Boss's new fans? Possibly, but it's certain that the two missing verses add to the complexity of the song.

'Johnny Bye-Bye' (Chuck Berry and Bruce Springsteen)
B-side of 'I'm On Fire'
On his *E Street Shuffle* blog, Ken Rosen speculates that Springsteen 'saw an opportunity to draw both a direct comparison and contrast between the fairy tale of Johnny B. Goode and the ugly demise of Elvis Presley by welding Berry's song onto his own.'

That makes sense. 'Johnny Bye-Bye' borrows the first verse of Chuck Berry's sequel to his hit 'Johnny B. Goode': 'Bye Bye Johnny'. Both songs are short: Berry's just over two minutes, Springsteen's just under. The songs are in different keys, but both are three-chord blues numbers employing early rock 'n' roll rhythm and instrumentation, with 'Johnny Bye-Bye' featuring Springsteen on guitars and bass and Weinberg on drums.

However, as Rosen points out, after verse one, in which Johnny's mother draws out all her money from the Southern Trust to send her son on a Greyhound bus, the stories of the two songs become very different.

Berry's Johnny goes from Louisiana to California, where he makes successful 'motion pictures out in Hollywood', falls in love, then promises to bring his new bride home and 'build a mansion for them by the railroad tracks'.

By contrast, Springsteen's Johnny never leaves Memphis. He's on the way out of town, to 'the promised land', aka, California, when he meets a 'little girlie with the red dress on', and they decide to go to a party. The atmosphere is ruined, though, when 'a man on the radio says Elvis Presley died'.

In the next verse, the speaker is a 'we' – evidently, we have shifted points of view. As 'the sky turned hard and black', 'we' see a dead man in a white Cadillac that seems to be serving as a hearse. Elvis's hearse was a white Cadillac, so we assume he is the one inside. Instead, in a weird bit of transmogrification, the deceased is apparently Johnny himself.

And yet in the penultimate verse, Johnny is no longer in the hearse, but has been found 'slumped back against the drain/With a whole lotta trouble running through his veins'. 'Bye bye Johnny/Oh, Johnny bye bye', the final verse announces, 'You didn't have to die/You didn't have to die'.

It's all rather confusing from a narrative standpoint, but from an emotional perspective, it's pretty clear that Springsteen is meditating on the potentially fatal risks of fame for rock 'n' roll stars.

'Stand On It' (Springsteen)
B-side of 'Glory Days'
Put the pedal to the metal, go as fast as you can ... stand on it. That's the message of the B-side of 'Glory Days'. It's a rockabilly number, driven by

Weinberg's drums and Tallent's bass, with Bittan playing some mean piano, and the Boss nailing a perfect 1950s guitar solo halfway through.

'*Stand* on it', with the emphasis on the first word, is a catchy phrase, and Springsteen comes up with some clever rhymes. When, in verse two, Mary Beth is racing to save the deed to her ranch, 'she hit the shift but she just couldn't get a *hand* on it'. That's bad news because in addition to betting the ranch, she had 'a *grand* on it'. In the third verse, Columbus discovered America 'even though he hadn't *planned* on it/He got lost and woke up one morning when he's about to *land* on it'.

Sure, this is just one more song among many in the Springsteen canon that is (mostly) about racing fast cars – Jimmy Lee and Bobby are speeding around the track in, respectively, verses one and four – but it's a fun take on an old subject and a solid B-side, worthy of its later place on *Tracks*.

'Janey, Don't You Lose Heart' (Springsteen)
B-side of 'I'm Goin' Down'
Originally written in 1979 and titled 'Every Day And Every Night', 'Janey, Don't You Lose Heart' could well have been the A-side of a single. Recorded at the Hit Factory and mixed by Bob Clearmountain, the song rides on a snappy piano and synthesizer riff, both played by Bittan. The chorus is simply the title sung four times, with Springsteen quickly crooning 'No, no, no, no' at the end of each line. However, those four repeated words, which also appear in some of the verse lines, constitute a memorable hook in themselves.

The verses retread old ground for Springsteen. Janey is full of 'tears' and 'fears'; when she comes home at night, she lies in bed and feels 'this emptiness'. However, as we learn in the third verse, the singer is going to make everything all right. He'll be there for her until 'every river, baby, it runs dry/Until the sun, honey, is torn from the sky/Till every fear that you've felt bursts free/And gone tumblin' down into the sea'.

It's not exactly top-grade Springsteen poetry, but those 'no, no, no, no's – made all the more appealing by Nils Lofgren's harmony vocals – just won't let up, and, like any good earworm, the song burrows ever deeper the more you listen to it.

'Santa Claus Is Comin' To Town' (J. Fred Coots and Haven Gillespie)
B-side of 'My Hometown'
'It's all cold down along the beach', Springsteen tells us, after Bittan's bell-like piano introduction, and a 'Ho ho ho' from Santa Clarence himself. 'The wind's whipping down the boardwalk', he continues before asking the band, 'You guys know what time it is?' 'It's Christmas time', we learn, Elvis Presley's favorite holiday, and the Boss seems to like it pretty well, too.

The recording is an old one, from a December 1975 concert at CW Post College on Long Island, but it's the classic E Street Band lineup. When Springsteen gets going in the first verse, Tallent's bass practically rips through the speakers, and Federci's glockenspiel and organ provide an appropriately festive backing. There are some fun tempo changes, and some hilarious response vocals from Clemons, who also plays the bells and blows a classic line on his horn.

Is this a novelty song? Well, yes, it always has been since it was first sung on the radio by Eddie Cantor back in 1934, during the Great Depression. But it's a song of hope and resilience. If we are good, 'for goodness sake', then Santa will bring us everything we want for Christmas. Our redemption may be temporary, but that's all Santa, or the Boss, has ever promised us.

Live/1975-1985 (1986)

Personnel:

Bruce Springsteen: vocals, electric guitar, harmonica, acoustic guitar on 'No Surrender'

Roy Bittan: piano, synthesizer, backing vocals

Clarence Clemons: saxophone, percussion, backing vocals

Danny Federici: organ, accordion, glockenspiel, piano, synthesizer on 'My Hometown', backing vocals

Nils Lofgren (beginning in 1984): electric and acoustic guitars, backing vocals

Patti Scialfa (beginning in 1984): backing vocals, synthesizer on 'Born In The U.S.A.'

Garry Tallent: bass guitar, backing vocals

Steve Van Zandt (through 1981): electric guitar, acoustic guitar, backing vocals

Max Weinberg: drums

Flo and Eddie (Howard Kaylan and Mark Volman): backing vocals on 'Hungry Heart'

The Miami Horns (Stan Harrison: tenor saxophone, Eddie Manion: baritone saxophone, Mark Pender: trumpet, Richie 'La Bamba' Rosenberg: trombone): horns on 'Tenth Avenue Freeze-Out'

Recorded at The Roxy, West Hollywood; Nassau Coliseum, Uniondale, New York; Winterland Ballroom, San Francisco; Meadowlands Arena, East Rutherford, New Jersey; Arizona State University, Tempe; Giants Stadium, East Rutherford, New Jersey; Los Angeles Memorial Coliseum: with additional recording at Right Track Recording, New York City; The Hit Factory, New York City; Record Plant, Los Angeles, between 18 October 1975 and 30 September 1985

Producers: Jon Landau, Chuck Plotkin, Bruce Springsteen

Release date: 10 November 1986

Running time: 216:13

Label: Columbia

Album charts: US: 1, UK: 4

Singles charts: 'War' (US: 8, UK: 18); 'Fire' (US: 46, UK: 54); 'Born To Run' (UK: 16)

True Springsteen fans had long insisted that the best way to experience the Boss's music was live at one of his concerts, and *Live/1975-1985* offers up the next best thing, a sprawling five-LP (later three-CD) set of songs. More than three and a half hours of music – about the length of a robust Springsteen concert – the box set showcases both the range of Springsteen's offerings and the rock 'n' roll that is always at its heart.

That said, this is not a thoroughly comprehensive look at the years 1975 through 1985. There is only one performance from before 1978, a 1975 recording of 'Thunder Road'. Where, devotees wanted to know, were the songs from the legendary August 1975 show at New York's Bottom Line? What we mostly get are songs recorded during the tours supporting *Darkness On The Edge Of Town*, *The River*, and *Born In The U.S.A.* Songs from the latter album are especially well-represented, with eight of its 12 tracks on *Live/1975-1985*.

In a rather bizarre 1984 *People* article featuring a conversation between Springsteen and Michael Jackson, the Boss explains why he's so loquacious in his concerts: 'I tell stories. People like that, I've learned. They like to hear your voice do something besides singing. They go wild when you just ... talk.' Not everyone is equally taken with this aspect of a Springsteen concert (raises hand), and thankfully, there is less talking and more music than one might expect to hear at a typical show – and far less than at a much later live recorded event, *Springsteen On Broadway* (2018), where the spoken stories vie with the sung songs for dominance.

Springsteen had insisted that it be his name only on the jackets and records of his studio albums, but he realized that, as a live rock 'n' roll act, he was only as good as his band, and this mammoth enterprise is credited to Bruce Springsteen and the E Street Band, a long overdue acknowledgement in the eyes of many fans.

While the original LP box set included a 32-page color booklet with lyrics and lots of photographs of Springsteen and his bandmates, the exterior was rather spare. The front cover photograph, taken by Neal Preston, shows Springsteen on the extreme left, holding his famous Telecaster-Esquire guitar. His sleeves are rolled up to show his muscled arms, and he wears black jeans and boots, which are almost lost in the footlights at his feet. He's staring off to the right, sweaty, presumably exhausted from performing. Most of the cover is black, with the full band credited above the album's title. The back of the box is even plainer. It's the same scene, but with no Boss. Instead, we see the list of all 40 songs with the place and date where each was recorded.

The album debuted at number one in the US and went to number four in the UK, but, as Rob Kirkpatrick notes in *Magic In The Night*, at this point some listeners were beginning to feel 'Bruced out': 'Ever since the hype heyday of *Born To Run*, Springsteen has been viewed skeptically by hipsters who view his – or anybody's – meteoric rise with cynicism. Ten years later, with the one-time rock 'n' roll future having become pop music's present, even those who had heralded his coming began to turn against Springsteen.'

Lester Bangs, in one particularly damning instance, compared Springsteen to Middle of the Road hitmakers REO Speedwagon. However, David Fricke in the ever-loyal *Rolling Stone* called *Live/1975-1985* 'an embarrassment of riches ... the ultimate rock-concert experience of the past decade finally packaged for living-room consumption.' And Stephen Holden of *The New York Times* defended the set as 'a record of how one singer and his band have helped to sustain and put their personal stamp on a rock tradition that has been steadily eroded over the last decade', saying it 'brings to a magnificent synthesis just about all the impulses that have fueled rock music since in surfaced in the mid-1950s as a mass cultural movement.'

Ultimately, the endless touring, the '1,001 nights of comradeship and good rockin'' Springsteen talks about in the booklet's liner notes, seemed to have worn out even the Boss himself. In *Springsteen: Point Blank*, Christopher Sandford quotes Springsteen as saying, 'We all sat there listening to [the box set] and sensed that it was the end of something ... next time would be different.'

Note: When considering the tracks that have been discussed in full earlier, I will focus primarily on their similarities with and differences from the studio versions. Songs that have not yet been covered will receive a fuller treatment.

'Thunder Road' (Springsteen)

Recorded at the Roxy Theatre in West Hollywood in October 1975, this is a variation of the classic Roy Bittan 'piano only' version of the song, although it also includes Danny Federici's glockenspiel as a delicate counterpart, along with Springsteen's harmonica introducing and concluding the song. Rather than exposing any weakness in the song, the stripped-down instrumentation makes it clear just how powerful 'Thunder Road' is from the ground up.

'Adam Raised A Cain' (Springsteen)

As if to showcase his and the band's range, the second track, also recorded at the Roxy, but nearly three years later, in July 1978, is the raucous 'Adam Raised A Cain'. This version opens with power chords before segueing into the short, brutal guitar solo. Bittan's piano is much more in evidence, and the band's 'yeah!'s following each repetition of the title are more pronounced. Steven Van Zandt's second guitar adds bite to a fully committed performance of the song.

'Spirit In The Night' (Springsteen)

'Spirit In the Night', from the same concert as 'Adam Raised A Cain', begins with Clemons blowing hard on his sax before Federici begins playing the riff on the organ. Everyone joins in on the response call to 'Spirits in the night', 'All night!', and the overall sound is much fuller, the beat steadier than in the *Asbury Park* original, with Clemons stealing the show not only with his solo but with his many fills. Springsteen milks the theatrics of the final verse, accompanied only by piano, before the band rejoin him to bring the song home.

'4th Of July, Asbury Park (Sandy)' (Springsteen)

Like 'Spirit In The Night', '4th Of July, Asbury Park (Sandy)' has been rearranged for a live performance. The sound is richer, though some of the nuances of the original are lost in translation. As on *The Wild, The Innocent & The E Street Shuffle*, Federici's accordion is a highlight, and Bittan attacks his piano part with relish. The song was recorded at Nassau Coliseum on Long Island in December 1980, and perhaps in deference to the hometown crowd,

Springsteen changes the line about Latin lovers 'Chasing all them silly New York virgins by the score' to 'all them silly New York girls'. In another emendation, it's no longer the waitress who has lost her desire for Springsteen; now, it's 'the angels' who have lost their desire for both the singer and Sandy, though 'every summer they ride their Harleys down from heaven'. It's a nice touch, and it seems to juice Springsteen as he sings the final chorus with gusto.

'Paradise By The 'C'' (Springsteen)

Writing in 'The E Street Shuffle', Ken Rosen notes that during the *Darkness* tour, Springsteen divided his concerts into two sets 'with an intermission to give feet and bladders some relief. That meant Bruce needed an opening song for the second set, something that would ease fans back into the show while late stragglers found their way back to their seats.' This is that song.

Recorded at the July 1978 show at the Roxy, 'Paradise By The 'C'' is an instrumental, a studio version of which would be one of the outtakes included on the 2015 box set *The Ties That Bind: River Collection*. Unreleased before *Live/1975-1985*, the song is a showcase for Clemons's saxophone – thus the 'C' in the title, with a nod to the pun on 'sea'. Federici takes a turn at the organ, and there are some lively guitar licks as well, but the saxophone is the dominant instrument.

There are plenty of Springsteen songs heavy with meaning and despair, so surely he's allowed this good time jam based on The Chiffons' 'So Fine' – a rollicking tune that would be very much at home in the Jersey Shore bars where the Boss cut his rock 'n' roll teeth.

'Fire' (Springsteen)

There are 20 seconds of subdued clapping and shouting before Springsteen announces, 'This is for all the girls here', then 'Fire', the song he wrote for Elvis Presley, begins its slow, insinuating riff. The performance took place at Winterland in San Francisco, in December 1978, less than a year after the infamous final Sex Pistols concert.

This is nothing like that. Instead of chaos, incomprehensible singing and a generally bad atmosphere, Springsteen offers up a moody, rockabilly rendition of the tale of a man who is besotted by passion for his beloved. The images are standard love song fare, far from the wildly inventive language on *Asbury Park* and *Born To Run*: 'You got a hold on me right from the start/A grip so tight I couldn't tear it apart' is hardly up to the standard of 'Thunder Road'.

Even the literary/Biblical allusions – 'Romeo and Juliet/Samson and Delilah' – are a bit odd for a song of seduction. Yes, 'Romeo and Juliet' felt a 'love they couldn't deny', but their brief affair didn't turn out so well. And Chapter 16 of the Book of Judges tells us that Delilah is 'an harlot' whose betrayal of Samson ultimately leads to his death. Very romantic.

The second song on side two of the original vinyl boxset, 'Fire' – at less than three minutes if you don't count the crowd noise on either end – makes the stitched-together concert feel as though it's dropped into a kind of eddy, at least for those listeners expecting a live version of a greatest hits album. Apparently, radio listeners agreed: the song as a single failed to crack the top 40 in both the US and the UK.

'Growin' Up' (Springsteen)

As we've noted, on stage Springsteen is a big talker, and this version of 'Growin' Up', recorded at the July 1978 Roxy show, adds almost five minutes to the original three-minute song. Most of the extra time is the Boss gabbing over Roy Bittan's piano and Danny Federici's glockenspiel. Springsteen's mother, father and sister are in the crowd that evening. He claims that for six years they've been following him around California, trying to get him to go home or go back to college – highly unlikely! – but that's not happening, he insists. In reality, it's a chance to reminisce about how unpopular he and his 'goddamn guitar' were with his father, and to tell the story of his motorcycle accident, and his parents' goals for him when he was a youth. Finally, he gets to the punch line, telling his parents, 'Tonight, youse are both just gonna have to settle for rock 'n' roll', and the band kick in so he can sing the song's final verse.

'It's Hard To Be A Saint In The City' (Springsteen)

While the *Asbury Park* version of 'It's Hard To Be A Saint In The City' always felt like a folk song dolled up as rock 'n' roll, the *Live/1975-1985* version, from the July '78 Roxy show, shows that the song really does have some rock 'n' roll bones. In fact, the centerpiece is a minute-and-a-half guitar battle between Springsteen and Little Steven – both come out winners.

'Backstreets' (Springsteen)

This rendition of 'Backstreets', rocking and passionate, adds a minute to the studio version, although it follows the basic pattern of the original. What's notable is that the 'Drive All Night/Sad Eyes' digression, a hallmark of the 1978 tour, was edited out of this version. Possibly that's because the song could well have run to 15 minutes, eliminating vinyl space for another song or two, although it could also be because Springsteen ad-libbing for minutes on end on a just a few lines doesn't necessarily make for scintillating audio without his stage presence (listen to but don't watch the Passaic 19/9/78 show on YouTube to test this theory).

'Rosalita (Come Out Tonight)' (Springsteen)

We're at the same Roxy show as Springsteen segues into a ten-minute version of fan favorite 'Rosalita'. You can barely make out the verse lyrics above the organ, saxophone and drums, but it doesn't matter: the audience already know the words, and the song is pure celebration, livelier, if possible, than the original.

The song was often the final number in a Springsteen concert, so it feels weirdly out of place this early in the five-LP set for the Boss to be introducing the E Street Band, with Clemons, 'King of the World, Master of the Universe', getting the biggest shout-out. Led by Clemons's saxophone, the band play for another few minutes before the song slows down to the final two verses about Springsteen getting 'the big bucks' and inviting Rosalita to join him in that little café down San Diego Way, with the final minute given over to pure rock 'n' roll jubilation.

'Raise Your Hand' (Steve Cropper, Eddie Floyd, Alvertis Isbell)
The third and final song on side three of the original album is a cover, one of just a handful on *Live/1975-1985*. It's the last song on the album from the *Darkness* tour, and the last song from the 1970s.

The lyrics of Eddie Floyd's original are fairly straightforward: the singer tells the object of his affection, in several different ways, that if she needs some love from him, all she has to do is raise her hand. It's a classic Stax soul song, from 1967, when the famous Memphis Horns were the driving force.

Eddie Floyd's rendition is 2:20; Springsteen's is 5:10. The difference in song length says a lot about how Springsteen approaches a live performance. He's always looking for that moment in the song that can open up and become a moment of communion between the rocker and his audience.

Springsteen's cover begins with Miami Steve Van Zandt offering up a brief Cropper-like guitar intro, then almost immediately, Clemons is tearing into the song with his saxophone, and it's clear that the 'lovers' the singer wants to raise their hands are the members of Springsteen's audience. There's a call and response between the Boss and the band, with the audience joining the bandmembers, and the whole song feels like a very communal experience. Indeed, the performance has the ambience of the culminating song in a gospel concert.

'You want to play, you got to pay', Springsteen informs the few people in the crowd who aren't standing. He then informs the listeners of the radio broadcast that is airing the concert to open up their windows and let the sound out to the larger world. We all need to raise our hands for what we want, he tells us. Amen, Boss, amen.

'Hungry Heart' (Springsteen)
The crowd on the opening song on side four sound much louder than the one at the Roxy, and that's not surprising, as we're back in the Nassau Coliseum in 1980. There are 16,000 people now, not 500, and the audience expectations are correspondingly higher.

Appropriately, Springsteen gives them the best-charting single of his career up to that point: 'Hungry Heart'. In fact, the song is so familiar to the crowd that

Springsteen allows them to sing the first verse and chorus without ever joining in. It's no doubt gratifying for a singer to have penned a tune with that kind of recognition, but it doesn't have the same impact on a record as it would live.

Fortunately, Springsteen takes over for the rest of the second verse. Federci's organ solo is the highlight of the tune, and the background vocals are strong, thanks to the participation of Howard Kaylan and Mark Volman, aka Flo and Eddie. Still, 'Hungry Heart, for all its upbeat vibes, remains, essentially, a pop song of its era.

'Two Hearts' (Springsteen)
The energy ratchets up even more as the next song was recorded in the 20,000-seat Meadowlands Arena in July 1981, with *The River* a number one album, and the entire population of the Garden State seemingly crammed into the stadium to hail their hometown hero. The cliché of the chorus – 'Two hearts are better than one' – with the awkward follow-up – 'Two hearts get the job done' – doesn't matter at all. The crowd are on board, and Weinstein's steady thwacking of the snare insists that Springsteen's vision of childish dreams ending only so that he can 'become a man and grow up to dream again' isn't just a lyric; it's the very Truth on which the Boss's life is built.

'Cadillac Ranch' (Springsteen)
The third song on side four, also recorded at the Meadowlands in 1981, keeps the straightforward rocking feel going. These 20,000 people aren't there to sit on their hands, and when they hear the familiar intro lick of 'Cadillac Ranch', you can feel the balance of control in the concert tipping from Springsteen and the E Street Band to the fans. As Springsteen sings about his love for Cadillacs – a cappella at first, then accompanied by drums – it's hard not to lament how feel-good silliness seems to have replaced the deeper, darker, edgier work that made him famous.

'You Can Look (But You Better Not Touch)' (Springsteen)
Springsteen has said in interviews that 'You Can Look (But You Better Not Touch)' describes the frustration of working-class people going shopping for items they cannot afford, and that's certainly true of the opening verse, but the second and third verses are about unattainable women, and the song feels more like a gimmick than a blue-collar anthem. Springsteen rushes through the lyrics as if he is embarrassed to be singing them, until mid-song, when, for more than a minute, he riffs on the two phrases in the title and 'Ain't nobody going to stop it'. Obviously, a concert is meant to be fun, and the first four songs on side four make it clear that Springsteen is keenly aware of that fact.

'Independence Day' (Springsteen)
Just when it feels as though Springsteen is intent on leading the world's biggest bar band, the last song on side four, and the fifth one from *The River*,

undercuts that premise. 'Independence Day' is played to the same raucous Meadowlands fans, and some of them even shout their approval when they hear Danny Federci's organ intro.

With a simple melody and forthright lyrics, 'Independence Day' is not only Springsteen's most moving song about his father, but it's one of the great popular songs about how children, inevitably, must travel beyond their parents' sphere of influence. Halfway through, Clemons lets loose with a short but tremendous solo that seems to summarize all the sadness threaded through the song, and in the end, the Meadowlands crowd gives the number the love it deserves.

'Badlands' (Springsteen)

'Badlands' was performed on 5 November 1980 at the Arizona State University Activity Center, the night after the election of Ronald Reagan. Does that make this version any different from the hundreds of other times Springsteen has performed the song? Sonically, it's hard to tell.

What we do get is a rousing account of the song, with Weinberg's implacable drumming pounding us from start to finish. But, of course, the lyrics themselves signal what's about to come in the following eight years: 'trouble in the heartland', a trouble that would continue mutating in the coming decades, ultimately resulting in Donald Trump's reelection in 2024, of which Springsteen would say in Manchester, England, in May 2025, 'Things are happening right now that are altering the very nature of our country's democracy, and they're too important to ignore.' Ultimately, he blamed 'an unfit president and a rogue government.' *Plus ça change, plus c'est la même chose.*

'Because The Night' (Bruce Springsteen and Patti Smith)

During his wildly prolific songwriting years in the mid- and late-1970s, Springsteen came up with the music and the title for a song. He couldn't seem to finish it, however, and when engineer Jimmy Iovine, who was working on Patti Smith's 1978 album *Easter*, told him he still needed a hit song, Springsteen gave what he had to Smith, who finished the lyrics and recorded her only hit single, which peaked at number 13 in the US and number five in the UK.

When Springsteen began performing the song, recorded here at the Nassau Coliseum in December 1980, he revised her verses. In interviews, Smith has said that she wrote the lyrics while she was waiting for a late-night phone call from her boyfriend and husband-to-be, musician Fred 'Sonic' Smith. Springsteen borrows some of Smith's wording, but his lyrics are both more working-man and less specific. To take just one example, the opening lines of Smith's second verse are 'Have I doubt when I'm alone/Love is a ring, the telephone'. Springsteen, in contrast, writes: 'What I got, I have earned/What I'm not, baby, I have learned'.

It's a rock 'n' roll parlor game to argue which version is best, but Springsteen certainly gave it his all on this evening. The song has a great hook, both musically and lyrically, and it's repeated frequently. Clemons has a short sax solo, and after a key change, Springsteen takes a much longer turn on guitar. Indeed, it's one of his most blistering leads, almost recalling the old days of Steel Mill, when he would solo all night long.

'Candy's Room' (Springsteen)

The third song on side five, 'Candy's Room', is from the July 1981 show at the Meadowlands. It appears to come as an encore, with the crowd giving a big *Whoop!* of appreciation, as though they have enticed the Boss back on stage. However, before the song begins, they start clapping rhythmically and fast, a response that is ill-suited for a song that begins as a piano ballad. 'Mellow out!' you want to yell at them, but then the song picks up steam, and you can no longer hear the audience over the E Street Band, who fully commit to the final two-thirds of the tune. Mad Max Weinberg machine-guns his drums, and Springsteen accurately reproduces his solo from *Darkness On The Edge Of Town*. His singing is throatier and more fraught than on the studio album, but otherwise this is fairly close to the song listeners already know.

'Darkness On The Edge Of Town' (Springsteen)

This rendition of 'Darkness On The Edge Of Town', from the December 1980 Nassau Coliseum show, is even closer to the original than 'Candy's Room'. That's just fine, of course, as this is one of Springsteen's best songs: it's in no need of concert adornments. Springsteen's studio delivery of his brave, heartbreaking lyrics is so passionate, it would be hard to top, but he does his best here, with the band showing us just what it means to want 'things that can only be found/In the darkness on the edge of town'.

'Racing In The Street' (Springsteen)

'Racing In The Street', the final song on side five, adds more than a minute to what is already a nearly seven-minute song. The crowd at the July 1981 Meadowlands concert go crazy when Roy Bittan plays the opening piano chords, and it is Bittan's piano playing that carries most of the song as the singer warbles what are surely the melancholiest lyrics about street racing ever written. The long outro is largely a duet between Bitan and Federici on organ, with Springsteen adding guitar grace notes to a lovely ending.

'This Land Is Your Land' (Woody Guthrie)

Springsteen announces to the crowd at the Nassau Coliseum in December 1980 that he's lately come across a book he admires: *Woody Guthrie: A Life*, by Joe Klein. He tells us that the song he's about to sing, 'This Land Is Your Land', 'one of the most beautiful songs ever written', was originally penned as an angry song in response to Irving Berlin's 'God Bless America'.

He begins with his harmonica, then fingerpicks solo guitar, as he sings the familiar words. Nearly two years before the release of *Nebraska*, the song's opening hints at what he could do working on his own. But this is a concert at a big arena after all, so he's joined by Bittan's piano and Federici's organ, and Weinberg's drums and Clemons on tambourine. They mostly drop out on the harmonica outro, leaving listeners with a sense of a very different Bruce Springsteen than the one they've been listening to so far.

'Nebraska' (Springsteen)

And then, in the very next track, we've jumped four years into the future, to the title song of *Nebraska* itself. Once again, however, you can hear the Boss's reluctance to present a song that was just fine with acoustic guitar and harmonica to a crowd hungry for the hits. The tempo remains the same, but the guitar is accompanied by a possibly overdubbed mandolin, then bass drum and those mid-1980s synthesizers that definitely make the song feel less timeless. It's admirable that Springsteen wanted to bring his less commercial material to a larger audience, but 'Nebraska' doesn't quite work at an arena show.

'Johnny 99' (Springsteen)

The performance of the next song, 'Johnny 99', also from *Nebraska*, takes us from the Springsteen who was a Big artist to the Springsteen who was Enormous, possibly the biggest rock star in the world at the time this version was recorded, in August 1985 at Giants Stadium, in East Rutherford, New Jersey, which has a capacity crowd of 80,000.

While the story 'Johnny 99' tells of someone 'who had debts no honest man could pay' and ends up with a 99-year prison sentence and a desire for execution is a gloomy one, the song is much more upbeat than 'Nebraska', and the protagonist has much more of a devil-may-care attitude.

The instrumentation is just Springsteen and his guitar and harmonica (with Clemons tapping on the tambourine at the very end), but the Boss delivers a huge vocal performance, and he seems genuinely committed to telling the story of a man who believes he'd 'be better off dead'. When the song is over, the crowd respond rapturously.

'Reason To Believe' (Springsteen)

And then we are back in the Meadowlands in 1984, and there is one more song from *Nebraska*. Like the previous three songs on side six, 'Reason To Believe' begins with just Springsteen, his harmonica and his guitar. But he's playing the electric this time, and in the second verse, Gary Tallent's bass and Max Weinberg's low-key drumming join in to give the mid-tempo song a dollop of energy.

A synthesizer enters in the third verse, and a second guitar on the fourth. Once again, Springsteen sings his heart out, as if he knows these mellower songs need him to sell every line. Harmonica and blues electric guitar take us to the end of what, by the standards of most bands – take *Yessongs* or *Wings Over America*, for example – would already be an epic live album. But there are still two full records and four sides of music to go.

'Born In The U.S.A.' (Springsteen)

The first track on the fourth record, 'Born In The U.S.A.', was recorded at the Los Angeles Coliseum, crowd capacity 93,000, on 30 September 1985. The band had been touring in support of the album for more than a year, and audiences by this time were wild for the Boss.

The familiar six-note riff sails through the air on a synthesizer, while Weinberg pounds out the steady beat and Springsteen practically screams the familiar lines. The music is so triumphant, while the lyrics are so full of despair: the quintessential Springsteenian paradox. A gnarly guitar solo toward the end seems to sum up those contradictions.

Less than a year earlier, Ronald Regan had been re-elected president of the United States in a landslide. The left-leaning Springsteen was doing his best to argue for a country in which working-class white people would become part of a broader coalition, like the one that would elect Barack Obama in 2008. However, back in 1985, it seemed that more of his fans were patriotically shouting out the chorus of 'Born In The U.S.A.' than listening to the verses in between.

'Seeds' (Springsteen)

As of this writing, 'Seeds' appears only on live recordings (to see Springsteen and the Band lay into it properly, watch the version on 2009's *London Calling: Live In Hyde Park*). That's a shame because while there's no chorus and the music is as simple as can be, this is a truly powerful song.

The narrator is a working man who has brought his wife and family to the Texas Oil Patch, but the work has dried up, and now he is living in his car 'on the streets/Of Houston town'. The lure of quick money has been replaced by a world where there are 'men hunkered down/By the railroad tracks', with 'tents pitched on the highway/In the dirty moonlight'.

Ultimately, the song takes the form of a warning to other northerners tempted to 'go on down/Where that sweet soda river flow'. According to the singer, 'You're better off buying a shotgun dead off the rack/You ain't gonna find nothing down here, friend/Except seeds blowing up the highway in the south wind'.

'Seeds' ends with a brief but wicked organ solo from Federici that quickly leads to one of Springsteen's angriest solos and then the full band, led by Clemons, giving their all to the three chords that have been thundering so insistently for the duration of the song.

'The River' (Springsteen)

Side seven comes to a close with another number from the 1985 concert at the LA Coliseum, an 11-minute version of 'The River'. Most of those additional six minutes come at the beginning of the song, when Springsteen tells an extended story about his conflicts with his father when the Boss was a long-haired teenager. That story morphs into one about the Vietnam War and Springsteen's successful draft dodging, which causes the crowd to clap, though he tells them, 'It's nothing to applaud about.' The punch line of the story is that when Springsteen tells his father the Army didn't take him, his father replies, 'That's good'.

It's a long way to get to one of his best songs, and considering the fact that 'The River' is about his sister and her husband, it feels oddly off-point. Fortunately, the song itself saves the track: it's a beautiful, heartfelt rendition that ends with a surprisingly up-tempo outro.

'War' (Barrett Strong and Norman Whitfield)
Side eight, still at the Los Angeles Coliseum, begins with an admonition to 'all the young people out there' – some of whom, no doubt, were young Reagan Republicans, hopped up on conservatism. Springsteen warns them that for the next war, 'They're gonna be looking at you.' And then, finally, he lays it on the line: 'In 1985, blind faith in your leaders, or in anything, will get you killed.'

The band then launch into a ferocious version of 'War', Edwin Starr's number-one hit from 1970. Part of the soundtrack for the anti-war movement, the song sounds even more relevant when sung by Springsteen to an audience who urgently need to hear that war is good 'for absolutely nothing'. Guitars wail, the band shout the chorus: this is Springsteen preaching at his most effective, and it's all the more satisfying that this song was the album's sole top ten hit, peaking at number eight in the US and number 18 in the UK.

'Darlington County' (Springsteen)
Where does a performer go in the very same concert after such a passionate, politically charged song? Well, in this case, it's to the country rock of 'Darlington County'. The song is lively and fun, but even with Clemons's extended sax solo, the comic narrative and 'Sha la la, sha la la la la' chorus of 'Darlington County' feel a bit empty after the fire of 'War'.

'Working On The Highway' (Springsteen)
'Working On The Highway', recorded at Giants Stadium in August 1985, starts off with some massive drumming by Weinberg that is soon accompanied by some distinctly understated rockabilly guitar beneath Springsteen's hurried singing of the lyrics. Tallent joins in on bass, and the synthesizers begin playing the riff, but the whole thing feels rushed, if not perfunctory, as though it were important to include yet one more song from *Born In The U.S.A.*

'The Promised Land' (Springsteen)
The fourth LP concludes with a brisk version of 'The Promised Land' that is memorable primarily for an inventive sax solo by Clemons and its long outro

over the band's 'Sha la la's. Overall, though, like 'Working On The Highway', this performance seems too fast, as though Springsteen had played the song one too many times to give it its proper due and wanted to get it over with as quickly as possible.

'Cover Me' (Springsteen)

The final LP begins with 'Cover Me', the second top-ten hit from *Born In The U.S.A.* Recorded at the LA Coliseum in September 1985, the song begins with a dramatic keyboard and bass buildup leading to Springsteen's new love interest, Patti Scialfa, singing the chorus of 'Nowhere To Run' by Martha and the Vandellas. Then Springsteen repeatedly pleads, 'Cover me!' 'I've seen enough', he wails, 'I don't want to see no more'. And then after a minute and a half of theatrics, the song moves to a duet between Springsteen and Scialfa on the final lines of the chorus that sounds very much like a declaration of passion. The normally three-and-a-half-minute song goes on and on for nearly seven minutes: when you're in love, sometimes a guitar solo is not just a guitar solo.

'I'm On Fire' (Springsteen)

Yet another top-ten single from *Born In The U.S.A.*, 'I'm On Fire' has an extended acoustic introduction, which leads to a moody, convincing reading of the song. Other than the occasional hooting and hollering from excited fans, the song isn't radically different from the studio version.

'Bobby Jean' (Springsteen)

As noted earlier, 'Bobby Jean', performed here at Giants Stadium in August of 1985, is often seen as a tribute to Springsteen's friendship with Steven Van Zandt, who, at this point, had left the E Street Band to be replaced by Nils Lofgren. The song is nostalgia-drenched, both musically and lyrically, with piano and, at the end, saxophone playing the melody. If Springsteen is, indeed, singing to his lost compatriot, someone who 'nobody, nowhere, nohow' will ever understand quite as deeply, then this is a fitting acknowledgement of that relationship.

'My Hometown' (Springsteen)

The final song on side nine, and the fourth in a row from *Born In The U.S.A.*, is 'My Hometown', one more top-ten single from the album – this version recorded at the LA Coliseum in September 1985. Forty years later, it's hard to picture a song this slow and introspective becoming a hit, although maybe Billie Eilish is a kind of weird avant-pop descendant of the Boss in this respect.

In any event, the synthesizer's wash, rather than sounding cheesy, actually gives the song some quiet grandeur. Federici plays the melody for the last minute of the song, drawing every last ounce of pathos from the story of a man who can never quite leave the blue-collar hometown that it seems will haunt him until the day he dies.

'Born To Run' (Springsteen)

The last side of the last LP begins with the Boss's Ur-number: 'Born To Run'. Recorded, naturally, at Giants Stadium in New Jersey, this August 1985 performance, released in 1987, went all the way to number 16 in the UK, though the studio version back in 1975 had only climbed as high as number 56. (This release didn't chart in the US.)

While Springsteen changes a word or two here, this performance of the song tracks pretty closely to the original, although synthesizers have replaced the old-fashioned organ. It's a great song, but is the studio version tighter and more impactful? Definitely.

'No Surrender' (Springsteen)

On *Born In The U.S.A.*, 'No Surrender' is an anthem of triumph: 'No retreat, baby, no surrender'. But Springsteen performs this version at the smaller Meadowlands Arena in 1984 with just acoustic guitar and harmonica. It's a sadder number played this way, with the title sounding almost ironic rather than victorious. These 'blood brothers with a vow to defend' sound like they would be more at home on *Nebraska* than on the mega-hit *Born In The U.S.A.*

Concerts present artists with the opportunity to fully rethink their songs, to bring out aspects of the original that were muted by the demands of producers and executives, or simply by the nature of the personnel gathered in the studio. Springsteen mostly sticks to his original vision of the songs on *Live/1975-1985*, but when he reimagines a track with real creativity, as he does here, the gamble nearly always pays off.

'Tenth Avenue Freeze-Out' (Springsteen)

The penultimate song of the set remains in the Meadowlands Arena in 1984, and the New Jersey/New York crowd are revved up to celebrate. Springsteen can barely catch his breath as he sings the made-up story of the E Street Band's origin.

The background vocals are big, as they need to be, but what really carries the song are the Miami Horns: Stan Harrison on tenor saxophone, Eddie Manion on baritone, Mark Pender on trumpet and Richie 'La Bamba' Rosenberg on trombone. The song demands brass that is tight yet swinging, and these four musicians are, like their predecessors on *Born To Run*, more than up to the task.

'Jersey Girl' (Tom Waits)

A standout track on Tom Waits's 1980 album *Heart Attack And Vine*, 'Jersey Girl' would seem to be a perfect fit for the Boss, and that turns out to be the case. It's also a great conclusion to this 40-song extravaganza, a celebration of all things Springsteen.

The song is a leisurely one, the sort of tune you might slow dance to with your baby in the wee hours in a small bar on the Jersey Shore. It's a song that sounds like it could be from an earlier era, so it's appropriate that it was recorded back in 1981, in East Rutherford, New Jersey. (The crowd go bananas when Springsteen says he's going to 'take that ride/Across the river to the Jersey side'.)

Waits's lyric focuses on how much he loves his Jersey Girl. When he's with her, 'all [his] dreams come true' and 'she thrills [him] with all her charms'. In short, he knows that 'someday she'll wear [his] ring'. It's an uncomplicated romance, but given just an edge by Waits's straining, growling voice.

Springsteen follows the first two-thirds of the song fairly closely, but he adds a final two verses to 'Jersey Girl', moving the song more into his own lyrical universe. Where Waits ends on 'Nothing else matters in this whole wide world/When you're in love with a Jersey Girl', followed by an ocean of 'Sha la la's, Springsteen takes us back to *The River* and 'I Want To Marry You'. His Jersey Girl is a single mom with a job that leaves her 'so uninspired'. His solution is to 'take that little brat of yours and drop her off at your mom's' and then to head out to a place on the Shore 'where the dancing's free'.

It's a convincing performance. Perhaps it's true: there's nothing quite like a Jersey Girl.

Bonus Tracks
'Merry Christmas Baby' (Lou Baxter and Johnny Moore)
B-side of 'War' in the US

'Merry Christmas Baby' was written by Lou Baxter and Johnny Moore in 1947 and first recorded that same year by Johnny Moore's Three Blazers, a rhythm and blues group. The original version, sung by Charles Brown, is slow and piano-forward until the break, when Moore plays a sly guitar solo.

The song, of course, has been recorded hundreds of times since then by everyone from Elvis Presley and B.B. King to Christina Aguilera and India. Arie. In addition to Springsteen's animated vocals, the E Street Band's live version relies on Clemons's saxophone and Weinberg's drumming for much of its energy. The song is a happy one, with the singer crowing that his baby treats him nicely, and he feels like he's living in paradise. There's a lot of vamping throughout, and a lot of interacting with an incredibly enthusiastic audience. It's fun without being essential: a perfect B-side.

In addition to being the flip side of 'War', 'Merry Christmas Baby' appeared on *A Very Special Christmas*, a quadruple platinum album produced by Springsteen's pal Jimmy Iovine to raise money for the Special Olympics. Other memorable moments on the album were provided by Madonna singing 'Santa Baby', Bob Seeger & the Silver Bullet Band performing 'The Little Drummer Boy' and John Cougar Mellencamp having a go at 'I Saw Mommy Kissing Santa Claus'.

Tunnel Of Love (1987)

Personnel:
Bruce Springsteen: lead vocals, backing vocals, guitars, mandolin, bass guitar, keyboards, harmonica, percussion, drum machine, sound effects on 'Tunnel Of Love'
Roy Bittan: acoustic piano on 'Brilliant Disguise', synthesizers on 'Tunnel Of Love'
Clarence Clemons: backing vocals on 'When You're Alone'
Danny Federici: Hammond organ on 'Tougher Than The Rest', 'Spare Parts' and 'Brilliant Disguise'
Nils Lofgren: guitar solo on 'Tunnel Of Love', backing vocals on 'When You're Alone'
Patti Scialfa: backing vocals on 'Tunnel Of Love', 'One Step Up' and 'When You're Alone'
Garry Tallent: bass guitar on 'Spare Parts'
Max Weinberg: drums on 'All That Heaven Will Allow', 'Two Faces' and 'When You're Alone'; percussion on 'Tougher Than The Rest', 'Spare Parts', 'Walk Like A Man', 'Tunnel Of Love' and 'Brilliant Disguise'
James Wood: harmonica on 'Spare Parts'
Recorded at Power Station and Hit Factory, New York City, between January and July 1987
Producers: Bruce Springsteen, Jon Landau and Chuck Plotkin
Release date: 9 October 1987
Running time: 46:25
Label: Columbia
Album charts: US: 1, UK: 1
Singles charts: 'Brilliant Disguise' (US: 5, UK: 20); 'Tunnel Of Love' (US: 9, UK: 45); 'One Step Up' (US: 13); 'Tougher Than The Rest' (UK: 13); 'Spare Parts' (UK: 32)

While Springsteen clearly enjoyed the success of *Born In The U.S.A.* and the touring that went along with it, not to mention *Live/1975-1985* shooting up to number one on the *Billboard* charts, he told *Rolling Stone* interviewer Jim Henke in 1982 that when it was all over, 'I just felt kind of 'Bruced' out.' Springsteen added: 'You end up creating this sort of icon, and eventually it oppresses you. So when I wrote *Tunnel Of Love*, I thought I had to reintroduce myself as a songwriter, in a very non-iconic role. And it was a relief.'

After giving himself over to the mixing and promotion of *Live/1975-1985*, Springsteen turned his attention back to writing and recording new work in January 1987. Unlike the endless sessions for *Darkness* and *The River*, *Tunnel Of Love*, Springsteen writes in *Songs*, 'happened very fast. Most of the recording was done over the course of three weeks. The writing was not painful, and though some thought so, not literally autobiographical ... For 20 years, I'd written about the man on the road. On *Tunnel Of Love*, that changed, and my music turned to the hopes and fears of the man in the house.'

The potentially autobiographical element was fascinating to both fans and critics because in May 1985, Springsteen had married his first wife, model and actress Julianne Phillips. As Rob Kirkpatrick writes in *Magic In The Night*, 'many might have expected a record (especially one titled *Tunnel Of Love*) that indulged in romantic clichés.' Instead, they got an album offering 'lyrical themes that hinted at the dangerous undercurrents of doubt and fear that live beneath the surface of love.' In *All The Songs*, Margotin and Guesdon refer to *Tunnel Of Love* as 'the divorce album', and, in fact, Phillips filed for divorce less than a year after the album was released, with their split finalized in March 1989.

Before all this happened, though, Toby Scott had installed a home studio in the room above the garage of the guesthouse of Springsteen's mansion in Rumson, New Jersey. Springsteen called the room Thrill Hill East. It was there that the Boss, much as he had with *Nebraska*, recorded his music, though with Toby Scott as engineer in place of the departed Mike Batlan. This time around, however, Springsteen had a 24-track digital tape recorder, a Sony PCM-3324, which gave him plenty of room to add color and range to his songs.

A photograph of the studio taken at the time shows the Boss playing a six-string acoustic guitar in front of the enormous digital recorder. Behind him is a 12-string guitar and a bass. On the far side of the Sony is a synthesizer and headphones. Atop one of the Yamaha speakers is a cabasa – a little extra real-world percussion to add to the LinnDrum drum machine that would be behind many of the rhythms on the album. A glass of pens rests inside a roll of duct tape on a cluttered desk. The picture is one any musician who has ever recorded at home will recognize, though this particular gentleman knows he will be getting a much larger hearing than almost anyone else making music in a similar setting.

With Springsteen playing all or most of the instruments on any given track, that left little room for contributions from the band, which was ironic considering how important the E Street Band had been to Springsteen's recent success, helping to launch him, as he puts it in his autobiography, into 'the big big time.'

Band members make guest appearances on a handful of songs, but there is no saxophone at all. Max Weinberg plays the largest role, but even he is only employed as a kind of session percussionist. In *The Stories Behind The Songs*, Brian Hiatt describes the process of Weinberg not playing drums but instead doing 'piece-by-piece overdubbing'. Weinberg would be 'sitting in a room with Springsteen doing little more than applying a stick to a snare drum with every other beat.' 'It was fun', Weinberg recalls, although he also acknowledges that 'it obviously was the beginning of the end of the E Street Band.'

The mixing was done by Bob Clearmountain at A&M Recording Studios in Los Angeles from May to July 1987. Whenever possible, Clearmountain replaced the LinnDrum's sounds with samples from recorded percussion, although the drum machine feel is present throuhout *Tunnel Of Love*.

The front cover photograph, taken by Annie Leibovitz, shows the clean-shaven Boss leaning against a white coffee-colored Cadillac, with the beach and the ocean behind him. He wears a white shirt and a black suit, with a black bolo in place of a tie. He's leaning to his right, looking suave, serious and handsome. His name and the album's title are on the top and bottom, respectively, in black font on a white background. The back cover is a slight variation on the front, with Springsteen, jacketless, leaning to his left and offering a trace more of a smile.

Writing in *Rolling Stone*, Steve Pond acknowledged the potential limitations of the album: 'energy rather than elegance is what sold *Born In The U.S.A.*; the scaled-down *Tunnel Of Love* is thus a chancier commercial proposition. The songs are the kind that many of the fans at the last tour's stadium shows talked through.' And yet, ultimately, he found it rewarding: 'One of the wonders of *Tunnel Of Love* is that in the end, he convinces us that the mystery ride just might be worth the toll.'

Robert Christgau was impressed by Springsteen's evolution as a songwriter: 'Where *Nebraska* was plunged in a social despair he never quite made his own, this companion piece comes out of personal compulsion. By depicting the fear of commitment as sheer terror, he does the impossible: renews L-O-V-E as pop subject.' This was the last time Christgau would award the Boss a straight 'A' for an album until 2018's *Springsteen On Broadway*.

Perhaps the most damning 'review' came from an old pal. After listening to the album, Steven Van Zandt was not impressed. In an interview with David Remnick for *The New Yorker*, Van Zandt recounts telling his friend, 'I'm like, what the fuck is this?' Springsteen responded that it was the truth about his own life. Van Zandt's rejoinder was devastating: 'This is bullshit. People don't need you talking about your life. Nobody gives a shit about your life. They need you for *their* lives.'

In the end, maybe both men were right. *Tunnel Of Love* went to number one in both the US and the UK, but it sold far fewer copies than *Born In The U.S.A.* Moreover, *Tunnel Of Love* marked the end of Springsteen's first great period of creativity. He would remain a rock icon for the rest of his life, but there were some relatively lean years ahead.

'Ain't Got You' (Springsteen)

If there were any questions about Springsteen's desire to make a clean break from his previous album, 'Ain't Got You' puts those doubts to rest. *Born In The U.S.A.* begins with a soaring synthesizer and mammoth drums, while the first song on *Tunnel Of Love* starts with an a cappella Springsteen, accompanied only by the faint snapping of his fingers. He's singing a homage to Billy Boy Arnold's 1956 rhythm and blues song 'I Ain't Got You', but Springsteen greatly exaggerates the things he possesses, other than the woman he desires. Arnold tells us he has 'a Eldorado Cadillac with a spare tyre on the back' and a 'charge account at Goldblatt', a now defunct department store. Springsteen, in contrast, claims to have 'the fortunes of heaven in diamonds and gold/I got all the bonds baby that the bank could hold/I got houses 'cross the country, honey, end to end'. Still, both singers lament: 'I ain't got you'.

At the beginning of the second verse, Springsteen begins playing acoustic guitar, harmonica, claves and maracas. These instruments are replacing silence, so they make a relatively big noise, though it's still very much a coffeehouse type of jam – informal, loose and fun. As the rockabilly number proceeds, we continue to get a catalog of the narrator's possessions, including 'a house full of Rembrandt and priceless art' and a 'big diamond watch sittin' on [his] wrist'. And he's not just rich in material goods. The singer is also desired by 'all the little girls' (there they are again) who 'wanna tear [him] apart', not to mention the 'hundred pretty women knockin' on [his] door', with 'folks' wanting to kiss him that he's never 'seen before'.

It's an odd song for a newly married man, but then again, even when he veers toward the autobiographical, the narrator in a Springsteen song is never really Bruce Springsteen. Still, his new wife might have appreciated something that seemed to be directed a little more squarely at her.

'Tougher Than The Rest' (Springsteen)

As the song begins, we hear Weinberg slapping the snare drum atop the drum machine beat while Springsteen plays something moody on his synthesizer, accompanied, beginning in the second verse, by Danny Federici's organ.

The lyrics tell the story of a man in search of a woman. It's Saturday night, and she's 'all dressed up in blue'. He tells her: 'I been watching you awhile/ Maybe you been watching me too'. He speculates that she may have been hurt in the past, but reassures her, 'Honey, I'm tougher than the rest'. He acknowledges in the second verse that he may not be a 'handsome Dan', a 'good-lookin' Joe' or 'a sweet-talkin' Romeo', but he's tougher than those pretty boys will ever be.

In the bridge, he continues to pledge his love to this woman he only seems to have encountered that evening, in a club, telling her he'd walk the 'thin thin line' for her 'any time'. There's a reassuring countryfied guitar solo, then the singer makes his final pitch: 'Well, there's another dance/All you gotta do is say yes'. It seems like a pick-up line for a one-night stand, although the heartfelt harmonica outro seems to want to convince us that the couple does have a chance.

If poor Julianne ever needed to have her fears confirmed about new band member Patty Scialfa's role in her husband's life, she only needed to take a look at the music video, where the sultry redhead sings directly into the eyes of her leading man, who sings straight back at her. Ironically, of course, Scialfa, not to mention most of the E Street Band shown in this concert video, do not appear on the album recording of the song.

'All That Heaven Will Allow' (Springsteen)

In the album's third track, we finally get a song that feels suitable for a new husband to sing to his new wife. In fact, 'All That Heaven Will Allow' is one of Springsteen's most openly romantic and optimistic songs.

Yet despite its head-over-heels approach to love, 'All That Heave Will Allow' – a bouncy pop song in which Springsteen plays guitars, bass and synthesizer to the unerring beat of the drum machine – manages to avoid sentimentality.

He does so through the humor and specificity of the lyrics. In the opening verse, he jovially warns potential competitors: 'Well, if you didn't look then, boys/Then, fellas, don't go looking now'. In the second verse, he's meant to meet his beloved in a club, but he claims to have left his 'wallet/Back home in [his] workin' pants'. He tries to convince the bouncer to let him in anyway, 'C'mon, Slim, slip me in, man/I'll make it up to you somehow', and with the sunny vibe of the song, we feel pretty sure the bouncer will comply.

'All That Heaven Will Allow' also avoids becoming sappy by, in the bridge, frankly addressing situations that might cause a relationship to falter. There will be 'Rain and storm and dark skies', to be sure, and the couple will encounter 'Mister Trouble', but the strength of their love will allow them to 'make it through you somehow'. And in the final verse, the singer renounces the dream of many a rock star early in their career: 'Now some may wanna die young, man/Young and gloriously', but that's not for this singer. His woman 'sets [him] straight and walkin' proud'.

Finally, the title itself works against sentimentality. Certainly, there is something heavenly about both his 'girl' and their relationship, but the length and extent of their happiness is under the control of a higher power. Heaven may allow them to continue on in their delight into old age. Or it may stop them dead in their tracks tomorrow.

'Spare Parts' (Springsteen)

'Spare Parts' begins with Springsteen singing, 'Bobby said he'd pull out, Bobby stayed in/Janey had a baby, it wasn't any sin'.

That's quite an abrupt shift from the lovey-dovey of the previous song, one that ensures the album will not be entirely about romantic love. And the music, led by the unrelenting beats from the drum machine, hammers the pessimistic message home. Aside from the title track, this is about as full as the instrumentation gets on *Tunnel Of Love*, with Federci playing the organ, non-E Street member James Wood playing a wicked harmonica and Weinberg thwacking his snare. 'Spare Parts' is Gary Tallent's only appearance on *Tunnel Of Love*, and his menacing bass shows that he's sorely missed elsewhere.

Until the very end, the story of Janey and Bobby is a miserable one. After they learn of Janey's pregnancy, the two are meant to get married. But Bobby is not like the narrator of 'The River', who stepped up into adulthood and got his 'union card and a wedding coat'. Instead, Bobby simply abandons ship, leaving Janey in a back room of her mother's house, walking 'that baby across the floor night after night'. Meanwhile, Bobby is 'in South Texas in a dirty oil patch'; when he hears about 'his son bein' born [he] swore he wasn't ever going back'.

'Spare parts, and broken hearts', Springsteen hollers for the chorus, 'keep the world turnin' ... around'. But what kind of a world is this, where unwanted children are described as 'spare parts'?

A potentially devastating one we learn in the song's bridge and penultimate verse. Having heard about another mother who drowned her baby in the river, Janey prays, then decides to do the same thing. Instead, when she is 'waist deep in water', about to commit infanticide, she looks up and notices 'how bright the sun shone'. Inspired, she lifts her son up, goes home, and in the final verse, vows to begin a new life as a single mother.

Bryan Garman may be overstating the case in *A Race Of Singers* when he argues that the song 'rewrites more than 30 years of male rock 'n' roll fantasies that celebrate the liberating effects of sexual expression but do not examine the power relations in which they are embedded.' However, it's clearly true that 'Spare Parts' is about Janey's empowerment, which, however, she only achieves by renouncing romantic love and becoming the sort of pragmatist who pawns her engagement ring for 'some good cold cash'.

'Cautious Man' (Springsteen)

Like 'My Father's House', a dream plays a significant role in 'Cautious Man'. And like Bobby in 'Spare Parts', this protagonist faces a crisis of commitment. There are also echoes of the 'Love' and 'Hate' on the knuckles of Robert Mitchum's character in *The Night Of The Hunter*, but Bill Horton, the hero of this song, is nothing like the vengeful Harry Powell. Instead, his own knuckles are tattooed with 'love' and 'fear', and until he falls in love with 'a young girl' he met 'in the early days of May', he is notable primarily for his measured response to every aspect of his life.

Once he does fall in love, though, Billy, 'an honest man', goes all in on his relationship. 'With his own hands', he builds her 'a great house down by the riverside', and 'He worked hard to fill their lives with happy days and loving nights'.

Nevertheless, Billy is also a 'man of the road', and he must pray for steadiness, knowing that 'in a restless heart the seed of betrayal lay'. His faith in his marriage is put to the test after 'a terrible dream' from which he awakes, 'callin' his wife's name'. In a panic, he gets dressed and heads out in the moonlight to the highway, prepared to leave his current life behind. In a 1992 interview with David Hepworth of *Q Magazine*, Springsteen summed up Billy's predicament: 'There's a world of love there and there's a world of fear, too ... and very often that fear feels a lot realer and certainly more urgent than the feeling of love.'

However, when Bill arrived at the highway, 'he didn't find nothing but road'. He experiences 'a coldness rise up inside him that he couldn't name', evidently a signal that he will always have to fight against the desire to flee domesticity. Yet, this 'coldness' also leads him back to his bedroom, where he brushes 'the hair from his wife's face as the moon shone on her skin so white', and the room is filled with grace and redemption 'in the beauty of God's fallen light'.

The instrumentation is muted, as is appropriate for a song where the lyrics take center stage. Once again, Springsteen plays everything. He fingerpicks his acoustic guitar and adds mandolin and some appropriately subtle synthesizer for this subtle song.

'Walk Like A Man' (Springsteen)
One of his most autobiographical songs, with references to places and events he would later mention in his autobiography, 'Walk Like A Man' also offers a tender portrait of his father, Douglas, with whom Springsteen had been trying to reconcile.

The first verse describes, in sensory detail, the interaction between father and son on the son's wedding day. The father's hand, placed atop the son's, is 'rough', and the son can feel his father's tears through his wedding jacket. That unexpected explosion of emotion on the part of his normally taciturn father spins the singer's head, and he tells his father: 'All I can think of is being five years old following behind you at the beach/Tracing your footprints in the sand/Trying to walk like a man'.

The second verse takes us back to Springsteen's first childhood home in Freehold, next to the parking lot of Saint Rose of Lima Catholic Church – 'By Our Lady of the Roses' – a house Springsteen valued as a boy and in memory for its trees: 'We lived in the shadow of the elms'. The rest of the verse, about the boy and his sister being dragged to the church to watch weddings, is also autobiographical, so that when the second half of the verse returns us to the singer's wedding, we feel he is giving a true account of the event.

The bridge takes us to the end of the wedding ceremony, and the last verse moves away from the newlyweds and focuses entirely on the singer's relationship with his father. The narrator admits that 'I didn't think there'd be so many steps/I'd have to learn on my own', and quietly accepts that his father is growing old – 'When I saw your best steps stolen away from you' – but the overall message of the song is one of reconciliation and harmony between the two formerly warring parties we saw in 'Adam Raised A Cain' and 'Independence Day'.

In *Rolling Stone*, Steve Pond calls the music 'as lovely an arrangement as Springsteen has ever crafted: a steady drumbeat with distant echoes of 'Racing In The Street', a gentle wash of synthesizer, a lulling melody.' Other than Weinberg's 'piece-by-piece overdubbing', all the instruments are played by Springsteen: guitars, a pretty good synthesizer solo and a bassline that has a spare, dignified groove.

Of course, one doesn't have to look too hard to see that there were more bad signs for Mrs. Springsteen. The song is primarily about the singer's father rather than his bride, and the answer to the question 'Would they ever look so happy again/The handsome groom and his bride?' would seem to be a big fat No. As Springsteen admits in *Born To Run*: 'When Julie was filming on location, I'd be at home in New Jersey, slowly slipping back to my old ways, the bars, the late nights – nothing serious, just my usual drifting – but it wasn't the married life.' Apparently, he had not quite learned to 'walk like a man'.

'Tunnel Of Love' (Springsteen)

Jason Stonerook points out in 'Springsteen's Search For Individuality And Community In Post-1960s America' that 'Tunnel Of Love', the first song on side two of the LP, is 'set on a carnival ride – an amusement typically enjoyed by adolescents – that serves as a metaphor for growing into a serious adult relationship.' The metaphor of the carnival is a tricky one. On the one hand, the narrator seems to be trying to transcend its hold on him and his lover. On the other hand, he does willingly immerse himself in its darkness. In any case, the song is hardly a ringing endorsement of adult romance.

'Tunnel Of Love' is the closest thing to an E Street Band song on the album. Gary Tallent and Clarence Clemons are missing, but Weinberg is doing his pared-down thing with the drums, Patty Scialfa sings background vocals and both Roy Bittan and Nils Lofgren play crucial roles in the song – although it's the drum machine that has the loudest voice during the first 20 seconds. Then, mercifully, Bittan's synthesizer comes swooping in with the hook, and Springsteen begins three verses and a bridge's worth of lyrics using a carnival ride to examine various aspects of love.

It's not a new idea, but the Boss's writing is quite effective. He opens with the grotesque image of the 'Fat man sitting on a little stool' who takes the money 'while his eyes talk a walk all over' the singer's female companion, as he whispers, 'Good luck with her'. Immediately, the singer tells his lover to 'Cuddle up, angel, cuddle up, my little dove'. Love in the first verse is primarily carnal.

While the second verse continues the emphasis on touch – 'I can feel the soft silk of your blouse' – when the lights in the ride go out, 'it's just the three of us: You, me, and all that stuff we're so scared of'. Love here is riven with fear and uncertainty.

In the bridge, love continues to be somewhat creepy – 'There's a room of shadows that gets so dark' – and yet there's also a comic side: 'There's a crazy mirror showing us both in 5-D/I'm laughing at you, you're laughing at me'.

Nils Lofgren's guitar solo adds significantly to the trippy atmosphere. His 'biggest showcase on any Springsteen studio record', Brian Hiatt writes in *The Stories Behind The Songs*, is 'a short virtuosic blast that sounds positively radical compared to Springsteen's own playing, complete with a quick Eddie Van Halen-style two-hand tapping part.' According to Lofgren, various foot pedals, flangers and choruses were added to achieve the psychedelic effect that graces his work in both the instrumental break and the outro.

The final verse acknowledges the difficulties of love: 'This house is haunted and the ride gets rough', though it ends on a note of determination reminiscent of that found on several *Darkness On The Edge Of Town* tracks: 'You've got to learn to live with what you can't rise above'.

For added realism, the screams at the beginning and end of the track were recorded by Springsteen's engineer, Toby Scott, at the Boardwalk at Point Pleasant, New Jersey. And the artsy music video, directed by Meiert Avis, is one of the better efforts at accurately evoking the mood of a Springsteen song.

'Two Faces' (Springsteen)

We learned on *The River* that 'two hearts are better than one', but two faces are most certainly not better than one when they belong to the same person. 'Two faces have I', the narrator sings four times, each time emphasizing his duplicity as a lover.

In *Born To Run*, Springsteen discusses his struggles with depression, which he feels were an impediment to establishing a meaningful long-term relationship with a partner. He was never in any sense schizophrenic, but the narrator's description of himself in 'Two Faces' is very much in line with someone suffering from bipolar disorder. The second verse is a succinct summary of the condition: 'Sometimes, mister, I feel sunny and wild/Lord, I love to see my baby smile/Then dark clouds come rolling by/Two faces have I'.

Despite all the narrator's failures, 'Two Faces', like 'Tunnel Of Love', ends with the singer standing up to Trouble. However, in this case, the trouble is himself, so it's hard to know which of his personalities will be victorious.

Other than a little percussion help from Weinberg, along with the ever-faithful drum machine, Springsteen is credited with playing all the instruments on the track: guitars, bass and synthesizers.

There are two solos in 'Two Faces'. The first, just before the final verse, is a heavily synthesized guitar line. The song ends with a lively organ solo reminiscent of the one on Lou Christie's dopey 1963 single, 'Two Faces Have I'. However, as Brian Hiatt points out, 'The credits of the album suggest that Springsteen played it himself, but it's so manifestly in the style of Danny Federici that either the credits are wrong or Springsteen managed to uncannily channel his longtime comrade.' Whoever is responsible for the outro, it both livens up the song and undercuts some of the seriousness of its reflections on mental illness.

'Brilliant Disguise' (Springsteen)

In *Born To Run*, Springsteen calls 'Brilliant Disguise' 'the center of *Tunnel Of Love*', claiming that the song 'postulates that when you drop one mask, you find another behind it until you begin to doubt your own feelings about who you are.' In that sense, 'Brilliant Disguise' is clearly a companion piece to 'Tunnel Of Love', where we heard about 'You, me, and all that fear we're so scared of'. Fear, along with desire, in the husband's case, seems very likely to have been the dominant emotion inspired by Patty Scialfa in both Julianne Phillips and

Bruce Springsteen. Indeed, it's easy to make a case that 'Brilliant Disguise' is addressed to either Julianne or Patty, or both, but, of course, the song tells us it is all about concealing one's true identity, so any autobiographical connections must remain speculative. Nevertheless, it's tempting!

In the opening verse, the singer holds the woman in his 'arms as the band plays', but even this putatively romantic moment is marred by the fact that the woman whispers something to him just as she turns away. Is it a vow of love, an admission of betrayal, or simply a request that he buy her another drink? Whatever the case, he saw her the previous night 'out on the edge of town', a location that we know rarely augurs any good. He tells her, 'I wanna read your mind to know just what I've got in this new thing I've found'. But in what sense is the relationship new? Is it the singer's new marriage, or a new affair with someone else? Or both?

The sense of possible betrayal, primarily on the woman's part, continues in the second verse. She calls someone else's name from underneath the willow tree in their yard, then he sees 'something tucked in shame underneath [her] pillow'. Maybe, he reckons in the final two lines, she's just too good for a man like him. The chorus continues his questioning about what is true and false: 'So tell me who I see when I look in your eyes/Is that you, baby, or just a brilliant disguise?'

In the bridge, the singer claims he is 'struggling to do everything right', yet when the lights go out and it's time for intimacy, 'it all falls apart'. After telling us that he's 'just a lonely pilgrim', Springsteen lets fly one of his oddest lyrics, 'I walk this world in wealth', which, for a moment, seems to take us back to the braggart of 'Ain't Got You', with his pound of caviar and fancy foreign car. But it turns out the line may be primarily to catch the end rhyme of 'I damn sure don't trust myself'.

In the final full verse, the narrator, if he is a substitute for Springsteen, seems mostly to be singing to Julianne: 'Now you play the loving woman, I'll play the faithful man'. But that's all a lie, and in the coda, Springsteen dives deep into the torment of his feelings: 'Tonight our bed is cold/I'm lost in the darkness of our love/God have mercy on the man/Who doubts what he's sure of'. Perhaps the singer is sure of his desire to be married, to walk like a man. More likely, he's sure that he's found the woman of his dreams, and she isn't his wife.

Along with Springsteen on guitars, bass and synths, a semblance of the E Street sound is provided by Bittan on piano and Federici on organ. This duo was truly remarkable, and it's great to hear them together one last time before Federici disappears from Springsteen's orbit for many years. In the rhythm department, Weinberg plays an actual fill just before the bridge, though the beats are mostly provided by the drum machine, and it sounds like it.

'One Step Up' (Springsteen)

Possibly the strongest track on the album, 'One Step Up' is a heartbreaker of a song, both for its simple, aching melody, and its description of a love gone sour.

Like any good poet, Springsteen conveys more by showing than by telling. In the first verse, after waking up to a cold house, he 'Checked the furnace, she wasn't burnin''. He has similar bad luck with his 'old Ford/Hit the engine but she ain't turnin''. These minor mishaps lead him to think that he and his partner have 'been giving each other some hard lessons lately', though they 'ain't learnin''. Basically, their relationship is 'One step up and two steps back'.

The second verse is even richer with imagery, with a bird on a wire outside the singer's motel room that 'ain't singing', and a 'Girl in white outside a church in June' when 'the church bells, they ain't ringin''. And then somehow the narrator has found himself in a bar, doubting his ability to grow as a person: 'I'm the same old story, same old act'.

The singer's refusal to lay blame on his partner is one of the reasons the song is so compelling. We see it again in the third verse, after he slams the door, 'Another battle in our dirty little war'; then he confesses, 'When I look at myself, I don't see/The man I wanted to be'.

In the final verse, 'There's a girl across the bar', and he's getting 'the message she's sendin''. In a great bit of Springsteenian description, 'she ain't lookin' too married', and neither, he admits, is he. But the song doesn't end with the two barflies hooking up for a one-night stand. Instead, the narrator tells us about a dream he's had.

It's worth pausing for a moment to register how important dreams and dreamers and dreaming have been in Springsteen's songs since the very beginning, from 'Mary Queen Of Arkansas' to 'The E Street Shuffle' to 'Born To Run' to 'Jungleland' to 'Two Hearts' to 'I Wanna Marry You' to 'The River' to 'The Price You Pay' to 'My Father's House' to 'Downbound Train' and 'No Surrender'. At times, dreams are places of refuge, but they are also spaces where the dreamer confronts his own delusions and wakes with an epiphany.

In the case of 'One Step Up', the dream feels desperate and ironic. The singer and his partner are dancing, just like they were at the beginning of 'Brilliant Disguise'. But this is a patently unrealistic dream, where 'the music was never ending'. The chorus has become dance steps, which we can imagine being repeated in the song's slow fade, as the dancers retreat ever further away from their goal.

Other than Patty Sicalfa, who sings in response to the chorus, then has a lovely vocal in the outro, Springsteen is the only musician on 'One Step Up'. The drum machine mostly disappears once the song begins, with Springsteen's delicate acoustic guitar complemented by a bluesy treated electric guitar, a well-considered bassline and some more than capable playing on the synthesizer. On this song, Springsteen holds his own without the E Street Band.

'When You're Alone' (Springsteen)
'When You're Alone' continues the theme of lovers falling out of love, though it does so in a decidedly bolder and more comic manner. The song begins

with the narrator telling us that his partner left him. (His name, by the way, is Johnny: no one will ever be able to say of Springsteen's characters, 'Johnny, I hardly knew ye'.) He doesn't seem especially broken up about her departure, calculating that her 'pretty form' will ensure that she gets along in the wide world.

Then Johnny offers up his philosophy on solitude in the form of a chorus. A listener's response to the song will be largely shaped by their appreciation (or lack thereof) of the heavy repetition in this refrain, which runs as follows: 'When you're alone, you're alone/When you're alone, you're alone/When you're alone, you're alone/When you're alone, you ain't nothing but alone'. It's easy to mock these lines as uninventive, but a more generous interpretation would recognize that the one way of emphasizing the feeling of being left by someone, of being truly *alone*, is to say it over and over again.

The second verse shifts to a different place and time, when Johnny was 'young and pretty on the mean streets of the city', which he fought to make his home. It wasn't an easy task, as he had only the shirt on his back, and he tells us: 'there's things that'll knock you down you don't even see coming/ And send you crawling like a baby back home'. During those times, well, you guessed it: 'When you're alone, you're alone'.

There's a very brief instrumental interlude, then Johnny seems to be having the last word, as his partner asks to return. He tells her he knew, 'You'd forget all about the bad and think only of all the laughs that we had/And you'd want to come home'. But that's not happening: 'it ain't hard feelings or nothing, sugar/That ain't what's got me singing this song/It's just nobody knows, honey, where love goes/But when it goes it's gone gone'. And there Springsteen, with his usual acuity, hits the nail on the head. When love disappears from a relationship, there is no getting it back.

Again, Springsteen plays all the instruments on this synthesizer-heavy, mid-tempo ballad. Kudos to his bassline, and to the background singing of Scialfa, Lofgren and Clemons, though the latter can barely be heard. Poor Clarence, one thinks: this is all Springsteen could find for him to do? In *Runaway American Dream: Listening To Bruce Springsteen*, Jimmy Guterman notes, 'It's the only time on the album that the band sing along; the irony feels intentional.'

'Valentine's Day' (Springsteen)

Rob Kirkpatrick points out in *Magic In The Night* that the final song on *Tunnel Of Love* is 'one of the few 'car songs'', which makes sense as Springsteen had declared he was no longer writing about 'the man on the road' but was now all about 'the man in the house'.

The narrative is straightforward: the singer, like so many Springsteen narrators before him, is driving a car at night and having deep thoughts. He is both anxious – 'one hand's tremblin' over my heart' – and happy: a friend 'became a father last night', and in his friend's voice, the narrator could hear 'the light/Of the skies and the rivers, the timberwolf in the pines/And that great jukebox out on Route 39'. (Brian Hiatt tells us that the friend who became a father was Springsteen's close friend and producer Jon Landau, who was celebrating the birth of his daughter, Kate.)

But the bridge returns us to darker musings, with the singer telling his beloved that he's not so much scared by 'the spooky old highway', but rather by the thought of losing her.

Then there's one final dream for the 1980s, with the narrator telling us: 'They say if you die in your dreams, you really die in your bed/But, honey, last night I dreamed my eyes rolled straight back in my head/And God's light came shinin' on through/I woke up in the darkness scared and breathin' and born anew'. The imagery continues, with the singer telling us it wasn't 'the cold river bottom' or the 'wind in the gray fields' that he felt rushing through his arms: 'No, no, baby, baby, it was you'. It sounds as though he's losing her, and, indeed, the final two lines have him pleading, 'hold me close, honey, say you're forever mine/And tell me you'll be my lonely valentine'.

'Valentine's Day' is a slow ballad, tied with 'Tunnel Of Love' for the longest song on the album. All the music is once more provided by the Thrill Hill East ensemble, i.e., Bruce Springsteen. Synthesizer chords and a loping bass are the musical interlude, and the outro is a line on the keyboard that sounds not unlike church bells ringing out on Christmas morning. For all its angst, *Tunnel Of Love* ends on a downright celebratory note. From out of the darkness, something good, surely, will come.

Bonus Tracks
'Lucky Man' (Springsteen)
B-side of 'Brilliant Disguise'

There's a third chord thrown in at the very end of the song, but 'Lucky Man', like 'Stolen Car' before it, is basically a two-chord song. In fact, it's mostly just a one-chord song, in E minor, with a four-note bass riff running through the number like some sinister secret being whispered by Old Nick. The beat is provided by a Springsteen-programmed LinnDrum drum machine. A synthesizer enters toward the beginning of the third verse, but the most notable sound is Springsteen's electric guitar, which accents the empty spaces between words with snaky, sustained notes.

This minimal instrumentation, all of it by the Boss himself, seems designed to highlight the lyrics, which tell the story of a man who is lucky because, as the narrator says, quoting from Rudyard Kipling's poem 'The Winners', 'He travels fastest who travels alone'. He does seem to be genuinely lucky in that, unlike his Pa, who went from the army to the factory to the killing yard, the Lucky Man makes his 'living with [his] hands behind the wheel of this car'. What exactly he is doing, other than driving from state to state, is unclear, but he seems to be almost constantly on the road.

Yet, there's plenty of room for irony. His need for incessant travel means the Lucky Man can never be in a long-term relationship. He tells us: 'Had a girl in

Calgary, I gave her up/Man, that love thing was messin' with my luck'. Later, addressing a different lover, he sings: 'I wake up tomorrow morning in another state/Kiss me now, baby, before it's too late/If you want to kiss a lucky man'. It's not the sort of luck everyone would crave.

According to Phillipe Margotin and Jean-Michel Guesdon, the song had been intended for the slot on the album reserved for 'Tunnel Of Love', but 'Springsteen changed his mind at the last moment, no doubt to preserve a consistency of sound.' It's hard to imagine 'Lucky Man' cracking the *Billboard* top ten like 'Tunnel Of Love'. Indeed, it would have robbed *Tunnel Of Love* of much of its character. As ever, when it came to selecting and arranging the tracks for his albums, the Boss's instinct proved correct.

'Two For The Road' (Springsteen)
B-side of 'Tunnel Of Love'

The flip side of 'Tunnel Of Love' is the opposite of that song in just about every way. While the album's title track is big, synth-driven, almost bombastic in its emotions and presentation, warning us that 'it's easy for two people to lose each other', 'Two For The Road' is a finger-picked acoustic guitar number assuring listeners that, to borrow from an earlier song, 'two hearts are better than one'.

The singer is addressing his sweetheart throughout the song, telling her, 'I didn't see it coming but, girl, now I know/It takes one for the running but two for the road'. 'A dream's just a dream in one empty heart', he declares later, pledging to her, 'When you're alone, my love'll shine the light/Through the dark and starless night/I'll hold you close and never let you go'.

The instrumental break features a gentle electric guitar, with Springsteen whistling the melody along with it. He also plays a subdued synthesizer, which remains very much in the background. 'Two For The Road' is a short song, but offers two heartening minutes of antidote to the troubled songs on *Tunnel Of Love*.

'Roulette' (Springsteen)
B-side of 'One Step Up' and 'Tougher Than The Rest'

Recorded during *The River* sessions, 'Roulette' was written shortly after the 1979 meltdown of Reactor Number 2 at Three Mile Island, near Harrisburg, Pennsylvania. In *Born To Run*, Springsteen describes 'Roulette' as 'a portrait of a family man caught in the shadow of the Three Mile Island nuclear accident.' According to Brian Hiatt in *The Story Behind The Songs*, after mixing 'Roulette', Bob Clearmountain asked Springsteen if he was planning to release the song as a single 'because it's so *topical*.' Producer Jon Landau, who was there, reported that the Boss 'winced as if it was a crass suggestion.'

That's a shame because 'Roulette' is one of the great Springsteen songs. It begins with some crazy rolls by Weinberg on his toms, then the band crash in and Springsteen plays the hook a couple of times on his electric guitar.

Weinberg smacks his snare with no-nonsense energy, and Springsteen and Van Zandt's guitars ratchet up the tension as the singer tells us, 'We left the toys out in the yard/I took my wife and kids and left my home unguarded/We packed what we could into the car/No one here knows how it started'.

Unfortunately, things just become more and more disheartening for the narrator. He wants some answers from the authorities, but he's not getting any, and he realizes that they are playing roulette with his and his family's lives. His home is his no more: 'There's a shadow in my backyard/I've got a house full of things that I can't touch'. He is now 'the big expendable', his life has been 'cancelled null and void'.

In the final set of lyrics, the narrator is arrested by police patrolling the area around the roadblocked accident scene. Somehow, our hero breaks loose, and now, on the run, with a metaphorical bullet 'spinning in the chamber' like a roulette wheel, he realizes he no longer knows whom to trust or believe.

Throughout, the energy from the band is remarkable. They aren't quite The Clash – they're tighter and a notch less ferocious – but as Springsteen snarls out his angry accusations, 'Roulette' offers solid evidence that the Boss was very much paying attention to what was happening in punk rock at the end of the 1970s.

Epilogue: Just To Say Goodbye

The years after *Tunnel Of Love* were not especially good for the Boss. His days as a top ten hitmaker were mostly over. 'Streets Of Philadelphia' made it to number nine in the US and number two in the UK in 1994, but its popularity was boosted by the fact that Springsteen won an Oscar and a Grammy for the song, which featured in the Tom Hanks/Denzel Washington film *Philadelphia*.

Fortunately, his albums did better than his singles. 1995's *Greatest Hits* was number one all over the world. Even critical duds like the same-day releases *Human Touch* and *Lucky Town* made the top five, and every album but the acoustic *The Ghost Of Tom Joad* hit the top ten in the US and the UK (*Tom Joad* made it to number 11 in the US and number 16 in the UK).

And the Boss's love life improved considerably. He wed Patti Scialfa in 1991, and they have been married ever since, raising three now-grown children. Springsteen, the man, finally achieved the family life that Springsteen, the artist, had been questing for so ardently.

Over the years, Springsteen became, in his own way, as iconic as his early idols: Elvis and The Beatles. Fans flocked to his lengthy concerts, and with the advent of the internet, every bit of minutiae from the Boss's decades-long career became fodder for fan forums. 'Get a life already!' someone on the Greasy Lake Springsteen fan page told another user looking for clarification about an obscure lyric. (I was there myself on the same errand.) However, the person added a winky face emoji, suggesting that they, too, have traveled down the endless road of Springsteenania.

On 23 September 2025, Bruce Springsteen turned 76, but even after completing a grueling European tour, he showed absolutely no signs of slowing down. That year, in addition to releasing the mammoth *Tracks II*, he finally dropped the famed 'Electric *Nebraska*' sessions. Oh, and did someone mention a 2025 feature film? As *Bohemian Rhapsody* did for Freddie Mercury, *Rocket Man* did for Elton John and *A Complete Unknown* did for Bob Dylan, *Deliver Me From Nowhere* lifted Bruce Springsteen from the merely legendary into the realm of cinematic immortality, although the movie proved to be more popular with dedicated fans than among the general public.

The Boss, in short, will be around as long as there is rock 'n' roll. No doubt, he will continue to release new music as long as he is able, but there will never again be a run quite like the one he had from 1973 to 1987. Those first nine albums will remain touchstones for every listener who is seeking the holy grail of popular music: something magic in the night.

Status Quo in the 1980s – Greg Harper
978-1-78952-244-0
Tangerine Dream in the 1970s – Stephen Palmer
978-1-78952-161-0
The Sweet in the 1970s – Darren Johnson
978-1-78952-139-9
Uriah Heep in the 1970s – Steve Pilkington
978-1-78952-103-0
Van der Graaf Generator in the 1970s –
Steve Pilkington 978-1-78952-245-7
Rick Wakeman in the 1970s – Geoffrey Feakes
978-1-78952-264-8
Yes in the 1980s – Stephen Lambe with David
Watkinson 978-1-78952-125-2

Rock Classics Series

90125 by Yes – Stephen Lambe 978-1-78952-329-4
Bat Out Of Hell by Meatloaf – Geoffrey Feakes
978-1-78952-320-1
Bringing It All Back Home by Bob Dylan –
Opher Goodwin 978-1-78952-314-0
Californication by Red Hot Chili Peppers - Matt Karpe
978-1-78952-348-5
Crime Of The Century by Supertramp –
Steve Pilkington 978-1-78952-327-0
The Dreaming by Kate Bush – Peter Kearns
978-1-78952-341-6
Let It Bleed by The Rolling Stones –
John Van der Kiste 978-1-78952-309-6
Pawn Hearts by Van Der Graaf Generator –
Paolo Carnelli 978-1-78952-357-7
Purple Rain by Prince – Matt Karpe
978-1-78952-322-5
The White Album by The Beatles – Opher Goodwin
978-1-78952-333-1

On Screen Series

Carry On ... – Stephen Lambe 978-1-78952-004-0
David Cronenberg – Patrick Chapman
978-1-78952-071-2
Doctor Who: The David Tennant Years –
Jamie Hailstone 978-1-78952-066-8
James Bond – Andrew Wild 978-1-78952-010-1
Monty Python – Steve Pilkington 978-1-78952-047-7
Seinfeld Seasons 1 to 5 – Stephen Lambe
978-1-78952-012-5

Other Books

1967: A Year In Psychedelic Rock 978-1-78952-155-9
1970: A Year In Rock – John Van der Kiste
978-1-78952-147-4
1972: The Year Progressive Rock Ruled The World –
Kevan Furbank 978-1-78952-288-4
1973: The Golden Year of Progressive Rock
978-1-78952-165-8
Eric Clapton Sessions – Andrew Wild
978-1-78952-177-1
Dark Horse Records – Aaron Badgley
978-1-78952-287-7
Derek Taylor: For Your Radioactive Children –
Andrew Darlington 978-1-78952-038-5

Ghosts – Journeys To Post-Pop – Matthew Restall
978-1-78952-334-8
The Golden Age of Easy Listening – Derek Taylor
978-1-78952-285-3
The Golden Road: The Recording History of The
Grateful Dead – John Kilbride
978-1-78952-156-6
Hoggin' The Page – Groudhogs The Classic Years –
Martyn Hanson 978-1-78952-343-0
Iggy and The Stooges On Stage 1967-1974 –
Per Nilsen 978-1-78952-101-6
Jon Anderson and the Warriors – the Road to Yes –
David Watkinson 978-1-78952-059-0
Magic: The David Paton Story – David Paton
978-1-78952-266-2
Misty: The Music of Johnny Mathis – Jakob Baekgaard
978-1-78952-247-1
Musical Guide To Red By King Crimson –
Andrew Keeling 978-1-78952-321-8
Nu Metal: A Definitive Guide – Matt Karpe
978-1-78952-063-7
Philip Lynott – Renegade – Alan Byrne
978-1-78952-339-3
Remembering Live Aid – Andrew Wild
978-1-78952-328-7
Thank You For The Days - Fans Of The Kinks Share
60 Years of Stories –
Ed. Chris Kocher 978-1-78952-342-3
The Sonicbond On Track Sampler –
978-1-78952-190-0
The Sonicbond Progressive Rock Sampler (Ebook
only) – 978-1-78952-056-9
Tommy Bolin: In and Out of Deep Purple –
Laura Shenton 978-1-78952-070-5
Maximum Darkness – Deke Leonard
978-1-78952-048-4
The Twang Dynasty – Deke Leonard
978-1-78952-049-1

... and many more to come!

Would you like to write for Sonicbond Publishing?

At Sonicbond Publishing we are always on the look-out for authors, particularly for our two main series:

On Track. Mixing fact with in depth analysis, the On Track series examines the work of a particular musical artist or group. All genres are considered from easy listening and jazz to 60s soul to 90s pop, via rock and metal.

On Screen. This series looks at the world of film and television. Subjects considered include directors, actors and writers, as well as entire television and film series. As with the On Track series, we balance fact with analysis.

While professional writing experience would, of course, be an advantage the most important qualification is to have real enthusiasm and knowledge of your subject. First-time authors are welcomed, but the ability to write well in English is essential.

Sonicbond Publishing has distribution throughout Europe and North America, and all books are also published in E-book form. Authors will be paid a royalty based on sales of their book.

Further details are available from www.sonicbondpublishing.co.uk. To contact us, complete the contact form there or
email info@sonicbondpublishing.co.uk